LAW AND TERROR IN STALIN'S RUSSIA

Printed by: EntaPrint Ltd, Cranleigh, Surrey

LAW AND TERROR IN STALIN'S RUSSIA

by

JOHN HOSTETTLER
JP, BA, MA, LLB (Hons), LLM, PhD
(London)
A Solicitor of the Supreme Court

Barry Rose
Chichester, West Sussex

ISBN 1 902681 36 3

By the same author:
The Politics of Criminal Law: Reform in the Nineteenth Century

Thomas Wakley: An Improbable Radical

The Politics of Punishment

Politics and Law in the Life of Sir James Fitzjames Stephen

Thomas Erskine and Trial by Jury

Sir Edward Carson - A Dream Too Far

At the Mercy of the State - A Study in Judicial Tyranny

Sir Edward Coke - A Force for Freedom

Lord Halsbury

The Red Gown: The Life and Works of Sir Matthew Hale

With Dr Brian Block:
Hanging in the Balance: A History of the Abolition of Capital Punishment in Britain
Voting in Britain: A History of the Parliamentary Franchise
Famous Cases: Nine Trials that Changed the Law

Published by
Barry Rose
Chichester, England

Contents

Glossary

Central Committee	Elected by the Party Congress, in theory it was the Party's governing body between Congresses but in practice both came to be dominated by the Politburo.
Cheka	Extraordinary Commission for Combating Counter-Revolution, Sabotage and Speculation. The secret police from 1917 to 1922.
Comintern	The Communist International.
Decrees	'Laws' sometimes passed by legislative enactment but more often administrative and individual's directives and policy directions of the Party.
Gosplan	The State Central Planning Commission from 1921.
GPU	State Political Administration. The secret police from 1922-3.
Gubernia	A Province.
Gulag	System of Forced Labour Camps.
Kolkhoz	A collective farm.

Komsomol	Young Communist League.
Kulak	A well-to-do peasant.
MGB	Ministry of State Security. The secret police from 1946 to 1953.
NEP	New Economic Policy from 1921 to 1928.
NKVD	People's Commissariat for Internal Affairs. Secret police from 1934 to 1946.
OGPU	All Union State Political Administration. Secret police 1923-34.
People's Commissar	Minister of the Soviet Government (1917-46).
Plenum	A full meeting (usually of the Central Committee).
Politburo	Elected by the Central Committee it was the most powerful body in the Party although eventually its members were nominated, and dominated, by Stalin.
Procurator	Prosecutor and legal investigator.
Revolutionary	Nominally courts of law they operated in Tribunals secret from 1917 and during the period of War Communism and there was no limit on the punishments they could impose.

RSFSR   Russian Soviet Federated Republic.

Soviet   Literally, a council. All soviets were
                         controlled by the Party.

Sovnarkom   Council of People's Commissars, in
                         theory the government.

USSR   Union of Soviet Socialist Republics.

Preface

In writing this book I have had in mind two aims.

Firstly, to examine briefly the theories of Marx, Engels and Lenin on the state and law and consider how far they were developed, or distorted, by Stalin and Soviet jurists.

Secondly, and principally, to consider the criminal laws and courts of Soviet Russia and how Stalin used them to pervert legality and enforce terror.

It is not my purpose to write a history of Stalin's Russia. There are available a number of books in which that has been done already – and done well. Nor do I wish to join the debate between the totalitarian and revisionist schools as to how far Stalin was in total control or was driven by social forces and Russia's cultural inheritance. Rather it is, within the context of the aims mentioned above, to consider a number of themes or case studies. These include:

(i)   Lenin's approach to law and terror and what influence it had immediately after the Revolution and in the period of War Communism;

(ii) the nature of law during the New Economic Policy and the genesis and impact of article 58 of the Russian Criminal Code;

(iii) what the Smolensk archives reveal about crime and legality;

(iv) how 'revolutionary law' was used in the collectivization war on the peasantry;

(v)   the various Moscow show trials; and

(vi) the Stalin Constitution of 1936.

In their writings Marx and Engels had little to say about the law. Moreover, what they did say was conjectural about a future society that they knew they were unable to foresee except, as they thought, in broad outline. It was fundamental to their thinking however that law had a class origin and served the interests of the dominant class. It was an arm of the oppressive state machine that was part of the superstructure of society. But they had no doubt that the state would 'wither away' after the proletarian revolution, and the law with it, along the lines set out by Engels in his *The Origin of the Family, Private Property and the State.*[1]

This theoretical approach was adopted initially by both Lenin and Stalin and by the early Soviet jurists. As a consequence, after the Bolshevik Revolution, tsarist law was outlawed and at first as little thought was given to providing a lasting alternative as was given to the principles of legality and the rule of law. In effect, in a real sense criminal law was abolished. Legally unqualified persons were appointed or elected as judges by Soviets and enjoined to dispense justice according to a deliberately vague 'revolutionary consciousness' which meant they did not have to concern themselves with legal forms, rules of evidence or prisoners' rights, but could sentence to imprisonment or death anyone they considered to be an enemy of the state. The result was that these men operated within a system of state-organized violence and a co-existence of 'law' and terror that was to persist for decades to come.

In time, however, as Bolshevik rule was consolidated, the demands of governing a vast empire and the need to secure legitimacy for its power forced the Communist Party to seek some form of socialist legality. But Marxist theory provided no

---

1. Friedrich Engels. In *Marx and Engels Selected Works*. (London, Lawrence & Wishart, 1950), vol.ii, pp.169-296.

important and lasting source of legitimacy for the regime. That is why Stalin projected himself as a theoretician of genius and he and his rule cannot be understood in isolation from the economics and philosophy of Marxism. However, the theory as such, as distinct from its implementation, impinged little on the lives of ordinary people. More importantly for total control, like all dictators Stalin sought a legitimacy sanctioned by law. Cromwell, Napoleon and Hitler did the same. However, it was more difficult for Stalin to adapt the law to his purpose since, according to Marx and Engels – enthusiastically endorsed by Lenin – bourgeois law had to be abolished and its successor, proletarian law, would wither away.

Stalin's Russia

What is known as Stalin's Russia is generally considered to have commenced in 1929, when Stalin assumed total power, and to have ended in 1953, when he died. Nevertheless, he was a member of the top Bolshevik leadership during the Revolution and became General Secretary of the Russian Communist Party in 1922. By that time Lenin's health was deteriorating and he was soon to die. Stalin donned his mantle in his devotional speech at Lenin's funeral and within the Party organization he was in a more powerful position than his divided rivals whom he picked off and neutered politically before eventually destroying them physically. Hence, to understand his use of the law and terror during the years of his personal dictatorship it is necessary first to examine the period from 1917 to 1929 that preceded those years and crucially stamped its mark upon them.

There are two reasons for this. In the first place because unlike some dictators who reshaped the law to their purpose the Bolsheviks who led the Revolution, including Stalin, abolished the existing law and replaced it with both legal and extra-legal repression that had a lasting impact. Law was not to be concerned with justice but was seen as an instrument of domination. And secondly, since Stalin's terror did not arise as it were out of the blue it is desirable to consider whether it was the consequence of one man's morbid paranoia, as those who think that Lenin would have acted quite differently like to suggest, or whether it was inherent in Marxist communism and the Bolshevik programme.

Stalin's Motives?

Stalin was directly responsible for the trials of specialists in industry, for the forced collectivization in the countryside and finally for the Great Terror. But his motives and whether he was pressurized by other forces, particularly social developments, remain the subject of vigorous controversy among historians. With a morbidly suspicious mind, did he in all these cases merely react to circumstances and suspected plots or did he ruthlessly determine to rid himself of potential rivals in the hierarchy of the Party and set on a course to create fear in the population and consolidate a totalitarian regime? Or perhaps both? Did he want not only power but also glory? And to what extent were his policies affected by pressures from below and within the bureaucracy?

These and other questions are much debated and there are various schools of thought. There is the Trotsky/Deutscher school based upon Marxist determinism which whilst not entirely denying a role to the individual in history sees the system as largely shaped by objective forces and interests. On the other hand, the totalitarian model favoured by Robert Conquest and Roy Medvedev has been widely accepted. And there are the revisionist social historians such as Sheila Fitzpatrick, J. Arch Getty, and Robert Thurston who play down the role of Stalin and the scale of the purges and believe the totalitarian model exaggerates the idea of a grand design. They want instead to stress the importance of pressures within society. Up to a point all these theories can be persuasive since by and large they do not attempt to deny the existence of the Terror. Where they differ is on its extent, on how and why it occurred and what its consequences were. However, one conclusion that might be drawn from Stalin's history is often overlooked. At times he was cautious, indecisive, opportunistic and pragmatic but it was in his nature to be dogmatic and cruel and this was reinforced, and in his eyes legitimized, by the ideology and practice of the state rule and terror that he inherited from Lenin. Yet no complete answer is likely to be found until the full range of Soviet archives are opened for research, if it is found at all. In the meantime whatever Stalin's motives and role the appalling tragedy that was Stalin's Russia, and the abuse of law in its unfolding, are clear.

Khrushchev – Opening Pandora's Box

Prior to dealing with these and other issues however, it makes a useful starting point to consider what Nikita Khrushchev revealed about Stalin's authoritarian régime in his secret speech to the Twentieth Congress of the Soviet Communist Party in 1956.[5] It must be remembered however, that in his speech Khrushchev was largely dealing with the terror Stalin launched against leaders and members of the Communist Party in 1935-38 and not his much longer reign of violence against large sections

---

5. For the speech in full, see Appendix 4 of his self-serving *Khrushchev Remembers*. (London, Andre Deutsch, 1971), pp.559-618 from which all the quotations here are taken.

of the population.

Khrushchev blamed everything on Stalin's 'cult of the individual' in order that he and his Party colleagues would not appear to be deeply implicated in what he called 'a whole series of exceedingly serious and grave perversions of Party principles, of Party democracy, of revolutionary legality.' And he accepted that Stalin had been transformed into 'a superman possessing supernatural characteristics akin to those of a god.' 'Such a man,' he said, 'supposedly knows everything, sees everything, thinks for everyone, can do anything, is infallible in his behaviour.' But he was careful not to say who had assisted in this chilling chicanery.

According to Khrushchev, Stalin originated the concept of 'enemy of the people' and 'against all rules of law' the only proofs of guilt used against persons so labelled were the confessions of the accused themselves which, 'as subsequent probing proved,' were acquired through physical torture. This led to 'glaring violations of revolutionary legality, and to the fact that many entirely innocent persons, who in the past had defended the Party line, became victims.' The Party, he continued, had available a large quantity of materials in the NKVD archives and other documents which established the fabrication of cases against Communists, of false accusations, serious abuses of socialist legality and the widespread shooting of innocent people. 'It became apparent,' he said, 'that many Party, Soviet and economic activists who were branded in 1937-1938 as "enemies" were actually never, enemies, spies, wreckers, etc., but were always honest Communists; they were only so stigmatized, and often, no longer able to bear barbaric tortures, they charged themselves (at the order of the investigative judges – falsifiers) with all kinds of grave and unlikely crimes.'

'How is it possible,' asked Khrushchev, 'that a person confesses to crimes which he has not committed? Only in one way – because of application of physical methods of pressuring him, tortures, bringing him to a state of unconsciousness, depriving him of his judgment, taking away his human dignity. In this manner were "confessions" acquired.'

The murder of Sergei Kirov (the popular Party leader in Leningrad) in 1934, said Khrushchev was surrounded by many things that were inexplicable and mysterious. Prior to the assassination the accused, Nikolayev, was arrested on the grounds of suspicious behaviour, but was released and not even searched. After the murder, when Kirov's bodyguard was being brought for interrogation he was killed in a car 'accident' in which no other occupant of the car was even harmed. Mass repressions and brutal acts in violation of socialist legality then commenced. Such acts committed before 1934 were left unmentioned by Khrushchev.

It had been discovered, he said, that of the 139 full and candidate members of the Party's Central Committee who were elected at the Seventeenth Party Congress (the so-called 'Congress of Victors') in 1934, 98 persons, i.e., 70 per cent, were arrested and shot in 1937-38. Investigations showed that all their cases were fabricated and that confessions of guilt were gained by cruel and inhuman tortures. Similarly, of the 1,966 delegates to that Congress, 1,108 were subsequently arrested on charges of anti-Revolutionary crimes and shot. 'This was the result of the abuse of power by Stalin, who began to use mass terror against the Party cadres.' And it happened after all oppositions had been defeated and socialist victories had united the Party.

Khrushchev then outlined the cases of a number of individual leading members of the Party who had appealed to Stalin and the Central Committee to investigate the tortures to which they were subjected but whose pleas had never gone beyond Stalin and the NKVD, the very people responsible. Lists of persons whose sentences were prepared in advance were sent by Yezhov, the head of the secret police (NKVD), to Stalin personally for his approval of the proposed punishments. In 1937-38, 383 such lists, said to contain 40,000 names,[6] were signed by Stalin and in one day on 12 December 1938 he signed 3,167 death sentences. Many of those whose names appeared on such lists have since been posthumously rehabilitated.

When some Party organizations, reported Khrushchev, complained in 1939 about the NKVD's methods of torture Stalin sent a telegram to Party committees in which he wrote that 'the Central Committee explains that the application of methods of physical pressure in NKVD practice is permissible from 1937 on, in accordance with permission of the Central Committee ... The Party Central Committee considers that physical pressure should still be used obligatorily, as an exception applicable to known and obstinate enemies of the people, as a method both justifiable and appropriate.'

'Only a few days ago,' said Khrushchev, 'we interrogated the investigative judge, Rodos - a vile person, with the brain of a bird, and morally completely degenerate.' 'The question arose,' he continued, 'whether a man with such an intellect could alone make the investigation in a manner to prove the guilt of people such as Kossior and others. No, he could not have done it without proper directives.' He told us, 'I was told that Kossior and Chubar were people's enemies and for this reason, I, as an investigating judge, had to make them confess that they are enemies.' He could do this, said Khrushchev, only through long tortures, which he carried out, receiving detailed instructions from Beria. Rodos explained that 'I thought that I was executing the orders of the Party.'

Khrushchev had a great deal more to say about Stalin but these glimpses of unbridled repression bear most directly upon the themes to be dealt with. Of course, much more has been

---

6. Roy Medvedev. *Let History Judge.* (New York, Columbia University Press, 1989), p.43.

revealed from recently-opened Soviet archives but Khrushchev, to his credit, made the first official breach in the once apparently impenetrable barrier of secrecy surrounding Stalin's methods of government by terror.

CHAPTER 1

Law in the Aftermath of the October Revolution

Marxist Theory

To the Bolshevik leaders of the Russian Revolution crime was a product of class society. This was in accord with Marxist theory but even so it is rather startling to find their *Programme of the Communist Party* adopted in 1919 proclaiming that under capitalism, 'The hungry masses stole to survive' (art. 2), and, 'The disgruntled workman protested his lot in murder and rape' (art. 11).[1] It is hardly a matter for conjecture how far this both reflected and coloured their view of the working class whose interests they claimed to be advancing. What is also clear is that they held the simplistic belief that socialism would provide an abundance of food and other consumer goods, as well as full employment, equality and dignity for all, and that as a consequence crime would vanish, taking criminal law with it.

This followed the classical Marxist approach to the state

---

1. See John N. Hazard. *Law and Social Change in the USSR.* (London, Stevens & Sons, 1953), p.85.

and the law expounded by Engels in a famous work, *The Origin of the Family, Private Property and the State.* In words that were to haunt the Stalin regime Engels claimed that after the proletarian revolution, classes would disappear and 'along with them the state will inevitably fall. The society that will organize production on the basis of a free and equal association of the producers will put the whole machinery of state where it will then belong; into the Museum of Antiquities, by the side of the spinning wheel and the bronze axe.'[2] To the founders of Marxist theory, law and its ideology were part of that oppressive state machine and would become obsolete in a more humane society. Indeed, Engels further said that the communists would 'put the axe to the root of crime – and thereby render the greatest, by far the greatest, part of the present activity of the administrative and judicial bodies superfluous.'[3]

Lenin on the State and Law

The early Soviet theory of the state and law was set out in Lenin's *The State and Revolution*, published in 1917.[4] A philippic against freedom and democracy it was based on the Marxist ideological view that the state and the law

---

2. Engels, *Op. cit.*, p.292.
3. Speeches in Elberfeld. *Marx and Engels Collected Works.* (London, Lawrence & Wishart, 1976), vol.iv, 248.
4. V.I. Lenin. *Selected Works.* (London, Lawrence & Wishart, 1937), vol.vii, pp.3-112.

are historical phenomena and form an integral part of the legal and political institutions of the superstructure of society which are determined by the prevailing mode of production (the base). In the *Communist Manifesto* Marx and Engels spelt out to the bourgeoisie that 'your jurisprudence is but the will of your class made into a law for all, a will, whose essential character and direction are determined by the economical conditions of existence of your class.'[5] Later, in *Anti-Dühring*, Engels was to write that 'the economic structure of society always forms the real basis from which, in the last analysis, is to be explained the whole superstructure of legal and political institutions.'[6] As such they served the interests of the dominant class in society.

So important was the question of the state to the Bolsheviks that in a lecture delivered in Sverdlov University on 11 July 1919 Lenin declared that it was the foundation on which the entire policy of the Bolsheviks had its roots.[7] He also emphasized that the state is a machine not only serving class interests but for upholding the *dominance* of one class over another by the systematic application of violence. Accordingly, Soviet law was to be an instrument of the proletarian state, not a limitation of

---

5. Marx and Engels. *Selected Works.* (London, Lawrence & Wishart, 1950), vol.i, p.47.
6. Engels. *Herr Eugen Dühring's Revolution in Science. (Anti-Dühring).* (London, Lawrence & Wishart Ltd., 1942), p.32.
7. Printed in *Pravda* (No.15) on 18 January 1929. Reprinted in Hugh W. Babb. *Soviet Legal Philosophy.* Cambridge, Mass. Harvard University Press, 1951), pp.2-15.

its powers. The dictatorship of the proletariat would not be bound even by its own laws.

Following Engels, Lenin stressed that whilst the bourgeois state would be destroyed by violent revolution, under the dictatorship of the proletariat, which in 1917 he was claiming would be direct rule by the armed workers and peasants, the new state would merely 'wither away' and coercion would become unnecessary since, in time, there would be no class dominating another. And this was not a promise for the distant future. The socialist state would be so constituted that 'it begins to wither away immediately, and cannot but wither away.'[8] Nonetheless, during the dictatorship of the proletariat there would be a series of restrictions on the liberty of the exploiters, and it was clear, he added, that 'where there is suppression there is also violence, there is no liberty, no democracy.'[9]

Elsewhere, he had said 'The scientific term "dictatorship" means nothing more nor less than authority untrammelled by any laws, absolutely unrestricted by any rules whatever, and based directly on violence.'[10] He did not add that since he himself had insisted that the proletariat would be politically slow to move without a vanguard to lead it, the dictatorship of the proletariat meant dictatorship of the Party, although on one occasion he proudly acknowledged such a dictatorship.[11] Nor did he mention that Marx, in his *The Civil War in France*, which

---

8. *The State and Revolution. Op. cit.,* p.24.
9. *Ibid.,* p.81.
10. *Works. Op. cit.,* vol.10, p.246.
11. *Ibid.,* vol.29, p.535.

drew on lessons from the Paris Commune in the spring of 1871, had said that the proletarian state should be based on universal suffrage, with representatives subject to recall, paid a worker's wage, and exercising both executive and legislative powers.[12] *The State and Revolution* was written just before the Bolsheviks seized power and contained its own contradictions, not least on the nature and function of the new form of government, but when Lenin was in control the repressive element became dominant over the 'unnecessary' coercion and continued to be after his death. As one writer has put it, the features of the authoritarian Soviet regime are present within every line and concept of Lenin's text. It's 'crime' is not that it did not work: it is that it did.[13]

Use of Force

In fact, one of the first measures of the Bolsheviks in power was to use force to shut down the elected Constituent Assembly for the convening of which they had long pressed. Indeed, the decree of 26 October 1917, which established the Council of People's Commissars, described the Council as a 'provisional workers and peasants government' exercising authority only 'until the convocation of the Constituent Assembly'. Similarly, the

---

12. Karl Marx. *Marx & Engels Selected Works.* vol.i. (London, Lawrence & Wishart Ltd., 1951), p.471.
13. A.J. Polan. *Lenin and the End of Politics.* (London, Mehuen & Co. Ltd. 1984), pp.129/30.

early Decree on Land which was crucial to the success of the Revolution declared that 'the land question in all its magnitude can be settled only by the nation-wide Constituent Assembly'.[14] But when the Bolsheviks found themselves to be in a minority, with only 175 of the 707 seats (when the Assembly met in the Tauride Palace on 5 January 1918) Lenin had its first – and only – session closed 'because the military guard is tired'. When its members arrived to resume their work the next morning they were prevented from entering the palace by armed troops.

On the day the Assembly met, unarmed demonstrators supporting it were shot at by Bolshevik soldiers, with at least 10 killed and many injured. Despite his warm feelings for the Bolsheviks, Maxim Gorky compared the event to the 'Bloody Sunday' of 9 January 1905 when Tsarist troops had shot into a crowd of peaceful demonstrators calling for reforms and killed 40 of them. He now feared, he said, for Russian democracy and that the fruits of the Revolution would be destroyed.[15] Confirming those fears Lenin said that 'the dissolution of the Constituent Assembly by the Soviet Government, means a complete and frank liquidation of the idea of democracy by the idea of a dictatorship. It will serve as a

---

14. *Sob. Uzak.* 1917-18, 1/1, 3. *Sob. Uzak.* is the abbreviated form of the pre-USSR *Collections of Laws and Regulations of the Worker and Peasant Government*. In Official Gazette, 1917-38.
15. Orlando Figes. *A People's Tragedy: The Russian Revolution 1891-1924.* (London, Jonathan Cape, 1996), pp.514-15.

good lesson.'[16] No doubt as another lesson, at the same time, on Lenin's initiative, the Constitutional Democratic Party (Kadets) was declared illegal, its members denounced as 'enemies of the people' and its leaders arrested.

A month earlier, in December 1917, Lenin had written that each village and town should find the means of:

Cleansing the Russian land of all vermin, of scoundrel fleas, the bedbug rich and so on. In one place they will put in prison a dozen rich men, a dozen scoundrels, half a dozen workers who shirk on the job ... In another place they will be put to cleaning latrines. In a third they will be given yellow tickets after a term in prison, so that everyone knows they are harmful and can keep an eye on them. (A lesson learnt by Hitler in dealing with Jews before the Holocaust and the Taleban with Hindus.) In a fourth, continued Lenin, one out of every 10 idlers will be shot. The more variety the better ... for only practice can devise the best methods of struggle.[17]

Terror thus became a compensation for, and alternative to, lack of popular support as it was deemed to be the only way to hold on to power which Lenin said they would never relinquish. Although he sometimes spoke of the need for strict observance of the laws such a sentiment always related to Soviet decrees which were either subordinate

---

16. Leon Trotsky. *O Lenine*. (Moscow, State Publishing House, 1924), p.24.
17. Figes. *Op. cit.,* p.524.

to, or enhanced, the use of force.

As far as legal theory is concerned, Lenin accepted in *The State and Revolution* that under the dictatorship of the proletariat there would for a time still be law – otherwise it could not 'wither away'. He put it that, 'In the first phase of communist society (generally called socialism) "bourgeois law" is *not* abolished in its entirety, but only in part, only in proportion to the economic transformation so far attained, i.e., only in respect of the means of production. "Bourgeois law" recognizes these means as the private property of separate individuals. Socialism converts them into *common* property. *To that extent*, and to that extent alone, "bourgeois law" disappears.'[18] But that was a forecast. The reality proved to be different and immediately after taking power the Bolshevik government proclaimed that bourgeois law was no longer valid, although Lenin conceded that the ideas of bourgeois law and social behaviour would remain in people's consciousness. However, the vital principles of 'no crime without a law and no punishment without a law' were rejected.

Perversion of Law during the Red Terror and War Communism (1917-1920)

The first Constitution of the Russian Socialist Federative Soviet Republic (RSFSR) after the October Revolution was

---

18. Lenin. *Op. cit.*

enacted by the All-Russian Congress of Soviets on 10 July 1918. It was largely drafted by Lenin and declared that the basic task was to form a workers' and peasants' dictatorship for the purpose of establishing socialism under which there would be no class divisions and no state coercion.[19] Supreme authority was vested in the All-Russian Congress of Soviets which effectively meant the Communist Party although this was not stated explicitly until the 'Stalin Constitution' of 1936. Liberty of opinion and association, freedom of meeting and equality before the law were 'guaranteed', but only for the toilers[20] which the Constitution said meant the workers, not peasants and others. The tension that would inevitably arise between these rights – for which in any event there was no machinery to secure their enforcement – and the dictatorship was bound to result in the dictatorship destroying the rights, as indeed it quickly did.

The Revolution occurred in only limited parts of Russia and with the support of only a small part of the population, and it was Lenin's policy of refusing to countenance a socialist coalition government, as well as closing the Constituent Assembly by force, that led in May 1918 to civil war and military intervention from the country's former allies. The latter supplied the Russian White Armies with arms, ammunition, equipment and occasionally troops but without making a decisive

---

19. *The State Constitution*. (London, The Labour Publishing Company Ltd., 1923), p.15.
20. *Ibid.,* pp.16-17.

difference to the outcome of the civil war. Their hostilities did, however, reinforce Lenin's warnings that imperialist countries wanted to crush the new state and this secured for him wider support and made a lasting impression. But the creation of a siege economy, and the openly declared 'Red Terror' that was formally proclaimed by decree on 5 September 1918,[21] were not simply a product of the civil war but were already part of Lenin's strategy for the dictatorship of the proletariat. Indeed, the Cheka had been formed nearly a year earlier.

His cold advocacy of violence was revealed as early as during the events arising from 'Bloody Sunday' in 1905 when, writing from exile, he urged that revolutionary squads be organized as military units. They must, he wrote, 'arm themselves, each man with what he can get a rifle, revolver, bomb, knife, stick, a rag dipped in kerosene for setting fires ... and so forth and so on.'[22] Whilst a law student Lenin had described himself in a report to the police as a nobleman but he had already been deeply affected by the execution in 1887 of his elder brother Alexander for an abortive attempt on the life of the Tsar. Although Lenin opposed assassination on the ground that whoever was killed would be replaced, even as a young man he had a good deal of sympathy with the violent aims of the People's Will Party with which Alexander had been associated. Indeed, although

---

21. *Sob. Uzak.* 1917-18. 65/710.
22. Lenin. *Collected Works.* (Moscow, State Publishing House, 1934), vol.9, pp.389/93.

personally he was not a cruel man he considered violence to be part of the evolution of society and his belief that terror was a means to educate and was a part of law, destroyed the ability of the state to exercise mercy to attract popular sentiment and sympathy.[23]

He also had a dogmatic and domineering character and a tendency to view the people as political cannon fodder for the Revolution around which his life revolved. As Maxim Gorky perceptively perceived in 1917, 'Lenin is a "leader" and a Russian nobleman, not without certain psychological traits of this extinct class, and therefore he considers himself justified in performing with the Russian people a cruel experiment which is doomed to failure.'[24]

Immediately after the declared Red Terror, on 11 August 1918 in response to reports from the Penza Region of a 'kulak' uprising, Lenin had sent a letter to local Communist leaders in which he said:

Comrades! The uprising of the five kulak districts should be mercilessly suppressed ...

1. Hang (hang without fail, so the people see) no fewer than one hundred known kulaks, rich men, bloodsuckers.
2. Publish their names.
3. Take from them all the grain.

---

23. Jane Burbank. *Lenin and the Law in Revolutionary Russia*. *Slavic Review*, vol.54, 1, Spring 1995, p.44.
24. Quoted by Orlando Figes. *A People's Tragedy: The Russian Revolution 1891-1924*. (London, Jonathan Cape, 1996), p.144.

4. Designate hostages.

Do it in such a way that for hundreds of versts (roughly kilometres) around, the people will see, tremble, know, shout: they are strangling and will strangle to death the bloodsucker. kulaks.[25]

The Red Terror

By the terms of the decree of 5 September 1918 inaugurating the Red Terror 'class enemies' were to be shot or isolated in forced-labour camps. According to Lenin, 'We cannot expect to get anywhere unless we resort to terrorism: speculators must be shot on the spot.'[26] In fact, two days before the decree Lenin had sent a memorandum to Nikolai Krestinsky, Secretary of the Central Committee, saying that 'It is necessary secretly – and urgently – to prepare the terror. And on Tuesday we will decide whether it will be through the Council of People's Commissars or otherwise.'[27] And, indeed, many thousands of people were killed in this early terror in which Stalin, whose ideology and methods mirrored Lenin's, participated. After all, to Bolsheviks the Christian commandment 'Thou shalt not

---

25. Richard Pipes. *The Unknown Lenin from the Secret Archives*. (New Haven, Yale University Press, 1996), p.50.
26. Lenin. *Collected Works,* vol.26, p.501.
27. Richard Pipes. *The Unknown Lenin from the Secret Archives. Op. cit.,* p.56.

kill' was simply a part of 'bourgeois' morality.[28]

If any doubts remain about Lenin's desire for murder, and his cynicism, his words in connection with Shuya, a textile centre near Gorky, should dispel them. On 19 March 1922 he issued the following instructions in a top secret memorandum to the Party's Politburo.

Whatever this involves it is now imperative for us to conduct the withdrawal of church valuables by the most decisive and speedy means possible; by doing this we can secure for ourselves an archive of several hundreds of millions of gold roubles ... Now and only now when people are eating human flesh in places where there is famine and hundreds, if not thousands, of corpses are lying on the roads we can (and therefore we must) conduct the withdrawal of church valuables with the greatest and most relentless energy, undaunted by any form of opposition in our path.

We must send to Shuya one of the most energetic, intelligent and efficient members of the Central Executive Committee, or other representatives of the central power and we must give him verbal instructions through one of the members of the Politburo. Essentially these instructions must indicate that the more members of the local clergy, local petit bourgeoisie and bourgeoisie he arrests in Shuya on suspicion of direct or indirect participation in violent opposition to

28. Nadezhda Mandelstam. *Hope Against Hope: A Memoir*. (London, Collins & Harvill Press, 1971), p.165.

the decree of the Central Executive Committee about the withdrawal of church valuables the better ... On the basis of [his] report the Politburo gives a detailed directive, again a verbal one, to the judicial powers saying that the proceedings against the people in Shuya who are revolting and opposing aid to the starving should be carried out with the maximum speed and completed only with the shooting of a large number of the most influential and dangerous members of the Black Hundreds[29] in Shuya; and wherever possible similar situations in Moscow and other spiritual centres should be treated accordingly.

The larger the number of members of the reactionary bourgeoisie and reactionary clergy we are able to shoot under these auspices the better.[30]

A Soviet historian has claimed that as a result of Lenin's instructions not only were the churches looted but more than 8,000 persons were 'liquidated'. The memorandum also clearly illustrates how trials and sentences were often mere formalities ordered by the Party in advance to facilitate the carrying out of previously arrived at political purposes. Stalin's concept of Party rule, in all its manifold aspects, closely followed that of Lenin as, indeed, did that of the other Bolshevik leaders despite their differences on tactics in given situations. Zinoviev, for example, as the

---

29. The Black Hundreds were anti-Revolutionary groups active in Russia in 1905-7.
30. Reproduced in *Izvestia*. April 1990.

Red Terror was launched told a meeting of Communists, 'We must carry along with us 90 million out of the 100 million of Soviet Russia's inhabitants. As for the rest, we have nothing to say to them. They must be annihilated.'[31] Ten million human beings to be destroyed!

Bolshevik Policy

At this time, industry was placed on a war footing, private ownership of land was abolished and special courts created. 'We need a state, we need compulsion' said Lenin now he was in power. 'It is the soviet courts,' he continued, 'which must serve as organs of the proletarian state effecting such compulsion.'[32] At this point the Communist Party became more centralized, it vilified and banned its allies, and introduced draconian measures against peasants, sailors and workers risings and, indeed, anyone considered to be a counter-revolutionary. Although the civil war exacerbated the situation this does not alter the fact that in general the measures taken, amounting to mass terror, were Lenin's chosen weapons and were in accordance with Bolshevik policy. According to Lenin in 1918, 'The revolutionary dictatorship of the proletariat is power won and maintained by the violence of the proletariat against the bourgeoisie, power that is

---

31. George Leggett. *The Cheka: Lenin's Political Police.* (Oxford, Clarendon Press, 1981), p.108.
32. A. Denisov and M. Kirichenko. *Soviet State Law.* (Moscow, Foreign Languages Publishing House, 1960), p.302.

unrestricted by any laws.'[33]

And his comrade-in-arms Nicolai Bukharin, in his *Politics and Economics of the Transition Period,* wrote that 'proletarian compulsion in every form, from firing squads to forced labour, no matter how paradoxical it sounds, is the way to create communist humanity.' Paradoxical indeed. He also quoted with approval Engels' remarks about the anarchists. 'Have these people ever seen a revolution?' asked Engels. 'A revolution is undoubtedly the most authoritarian thing imaginable. A revolution is an act in which part of the population imposes its will on the other part by means of *guns, bayonets and cannons.*'[34] Not surprisingly, legality and the rule of law were at a premium and law was not permitted, then or after, to limit the power of the state over the lives, and deaths, of millions of individuals.

What Lenin had said earlier about law soon disappearing after a socialist revolution was no longer interpreted to apply to criminal law which he saw as an arm of the terror, and during, and in the aftermath of, the civil war decrees required judges to administer justice, but only in accordance with their 'revolutionary consciousness'[35] as guided by the Party. This deliberately imprecise formulation was described by M.A. Reisner, of

---

33. Lenin. *Selected Works. Op. cit.,* p.123. It must be said however that at other times he called for strict observance of Soviet laws.
34. Bukharin. *The Theory of the Dictatorship of the Proletariat* (1919) in his *Politics and Economics of the Transition Period.* (London, Routledge & Kegan Paul, 1979), p.39.
35. For example, decree of 2 November 1917. 1 *Sob. Uzak.* 4/50.

the Commissariat of Justice, as 'nothing other than an intuition which lay at the foundation of the Soviet legal order'.[36] It was to be followed later in Germany with the 'Healthy *Volk* perception' used to determine guilt. When in a case of bribery the revolutionary tribunal in Moscow inflicted a punishment of six-months' imprisonment, Lenin wrote to the Central Committee on 4 May 1918 calling for the expulsion of the judges from the Party on the ground that the penalty should have been death by shooting.[37]

The Cheka

As early as 20 December 1917, months before the outbreak of the civil war, Lenin had encouraged the fanatical Bolshevik, Felix Dzerzhinsky, in having the largely autonomous Cheka (Russian Extraordinary Commission to Combat Counter- Revolution and Sabotage) created by resolution of the Council of People's Commissars. No legal decree was involved and to that extent the Cheka was an illegal body. Lenin knew this, of course, and the resolution was not made public until 1924, and then only in a falsified and incomplete version.[38] As its title indicates the Cheka was to deal with 'counter-revolutionary activities',

---

36. Hugh W. Babb. *Soviet Legal Philosophy*. Introduction by John N. Hazard. (Cambridge, Mass. Harvard University Press, 1951), p.xxvi.

37. Ivo Lapenna. *Lenin, Law and Legality*. In Leonard Shapiro and Peter Reddaway, eds. *Lenin, the Man, the Theorist, the Leader: A Reappraisal*. (London, Pall Mall Press, 1967), pp.260-1.

38. Richard Pipes. *The Russian Revolution, 1899-1919. Op. cit.*, p.800.

but these were held to include looting, hooliganism and black market dealings. Whilst the revolutionary tribunals which had been established in November 1917 purported to be courts (Bukharin called them 'the normal law-courts of the proletarian state'[39]), despite there being no established laws, their proceedings being held in secret and there being no limits on the punishments they could inflict,[40] the Cheka was openly promoted to be an administrative body without any legal rules at all.

At first the Cheka's duties were intended to be limited to preliminary investigations with victims turned over to the revolutionary tribunals but on 24 February 1918 it extended its tasks to include arrests and executions without any reference at all to the revolutionary tribunals. And, on 3 September 1918, *Izvestia* carried a telegram from Stalin who, not to be outdone by Lenin, called for 'open, mass, systematic terror against the bourgeoisie and its agents'. Soon afterwards Stalin became the Politburo's representative on the Cheka Collegium.

In effect, the Cheka treated all domestic opposition as treason and it was responsible only to the Party, for which it was said to be both 'sword and shield'.[41] It took for its headquarters an old insurance company building in

---

39. *The ABC of Communism: A Popular Explanation of the Programme of the Communist Party of Russia.* (London, The Communist Party of Great Britain, 1922), p.223.
40. Decree on Revolutionary Tribunals, article 1. 12 April 1919. *Sob. Uzak.* 1919/132.
41. John J. Dziak. *Chekisty. A History of the KGB.* (Lexington, Mass. Lexington Books, 1988), p.16.

Moscow called the Lubyanka, a name that was to become synonymous with prison brutality. Here, by June 1918, it had incorporated its own 'inner prison' and already controlled over 1,000 operatives. Eight months later it boasted at least 37,000, most of them troops.[42]

In the early days when the Left Socialist Revolutionary Party was for a short time in coalition in government with the Bolsheviks they to some extent held the political police in check, particularly when, for a short period, one of its members, Isaac Steinberg, was Commissar of Justice. He wanted in all cases persons in detention to be committed for court proceedings or released, but not surprisingly he was ignored. In his memoirs he wrote that he objected to Lenin's order providing for opponents of the government to be 'destroyed on the spot' for undefined crimes to which Lenin had replied, 'Herein lies true revolutionary pathos. Do you really believe that we can be victorious without the very cruelest revolutionary terror?' At this point Steinberg recalled he had called out in exasperation, 'Then why do we bother with a Commissariat of Justice? Let's call it frankly the *Commissariat for Social Extermination* and be done with it! Lenin's face brightened and he replied, "Well put! ... that's exactly what it should be ... but we can't say that".[43] Steinberg, who rightly considered himself a restraining influence on the Cheka, resigned as Commissar of Justice when the Left Socialist

---

42. George Leggett. *The Cheka: Lenin's Political Police.* Oxford, Clarendon Press, 1981), p.100.
43. Isaac Steinberg. *In the Workshop of the Revolution.* (London, Victor Gollancz Ltd., 1955), p.145.

Revolutionary Party left the government on the signing of the Brest-Litovsk treaty with Germany.

In the context of atrocities by both sides in the civil war and the allied intervention, the Cheka stepped up its system of hostage-taking and of mass executions of innocent people in batches as 'class enemies'. Concern at the Cheka setting itself above the law now began to be expressed, even in Party circles. At the Second All-Russian Conference of Commissars of Justice held in Moscow on 2-6 July 1918 one member perceptively saw the danger of a 'state within a state' arising and another quoted the president of the Cheka in Orel saying, 'I am responsible to no one; my powers are such that I can shoot anybody.' The reply of the new Bolshevik Commissar of Justice, Nicolai Krestinsky, concluded with the words, 'the work of justice must take a secondary place, and its sphere of activity must be considerably curtailed.'[44]

A year later, speaking for the idealists in the Party, Bukharin, who at that stage was a strong supporter of the Red Terror, was to say that the Cheka, the revolutionary tribunals and other instruments created for the critical period of the civil war were transient and would disappear when the counter- revolution had been crushed.[45] But he ignored the fact that the Cheka was formed months before the civil war erupted and, as with other ideas of his, how wrong events were to prove this prediction to be.

---

44. Merle Fainsod. *How Russia is Ruled*. (Cambridge, Mass. Harvard University Press, 1967), p.427.
45. Bukharin and Preobrazhensky. *The ABC of Communism. Op. cit.*, p.227.

In March 1920, the Cheka was authorized to sentence people to up to five years in its own labour camps by administrative decision if the investigation did not 'reveal sufficient evidence' for judicial proceedings.[46] Furthermore, widening its net, Dzerzhinsky said that the Cheka's concentration camps would be used to punish those guilty of 'an irresponsible attitude to work and for disorderliness and unpunctuality'. Thus was the dictatorship already turning against the very people in whose name it was said to be operating. Indeed, Bukharin, in his *Economics of the Transition Period,* elevated this to theory by arguing that when substantial numbers of workers resisted necessary measures of the state they did so against the long-term interests of the proletariat and to force them to comply with these measures was to force them to realize their own true interests.[47]

In the meantime some of the Cheka's tortures were so terrifying and horrendous as to be almost unmentionable, but for the interested reader they are described in George Leggett's *The Cheka: Lenin's Political Police.*[48] And although the Second Congress of Soviets had formally abolished the death penalty in accordance with a deep-rooted tradition in Russia going back to Catherine

---

46. *RSFSR Laws,* 1920. 22,23; 115. Quoted in Robert Conquest (ed.). *Justice and the Legal System in the USSR.* (London, The Bodley Head, 1968), p.8.
47. Neil Harding. *Authority, Power and the State, 1916-20.* In T.H. Rigby & Others. *Authority, Power and Policy in the USSR.* (London, The Macmillan Press Ltd., 1980), p.51.
48. *Op. cit.,* pp.197-8. See also Orlando Figes. *A People's Tragedy: the Russian Revolution 1891-1924.* (London, Jonathan Cape, 1996), p.646.

the Great, it had continued in practice and Lenin succeeded in having it formally restored in June 1918. In this connection it is worthy of note that the programme of the German Communist Party drafted by Rosa Luxemburg in December 1918 specifically rejected terror, emphasizing that, 'In bourgeois revolutions the shedding of blood, terror and political murder were the indispensable weapons of the rising classes. The proletarian Revolution needs for its purposes no terror, it hates and abominates murder.'[49]

Officially the number of executions carried out by the Cheka was 280,000 but, according to Leggett, other sources put it at half a million in Lenin's lifetime. In these ways the Cheka laid the groundwork for Stalin's adoption of the term 'enemies of the people' and their methods of torture to facilitate his even more bloody terror in the 1930s. Regrettably, but understandably, the Cheka's archives were destroyed in the early 1920s on Lenin's orders.

State Power

After the Revolution the Congress of Soviets had become in name the supreme body of state power, but in fact its powers were largely exercised by the Party-controlled Central Executive Committee of 200 members and this was confirmed by the Constitution. The actual government, consisting of the Council of People's Commissars

---

49. E.H. Carr. *A History of Soviet Russia: The Bolshevik Revolution 1917-1923*, vol.1. (London, Macmillan & Co. Ltd., 1964), p.155.

(Ministers), was responsible to this Central Executive Committee. At the Sixth Party Congress, which met in Petrograd from 26 July to 3 August 1917, Lenin had explicitly rejected the Western concept of the separation of legislative, executive and judicial powers and in consequence, policy directives might come from legislative enactments, administrative regulations, individual's decrees and, above all, policy directions of the Communist Party – and this was to remain the case throughout the Stalin years and beyond. The first Soviet Constitution, in July 1918, confirmed the arrangements mentioned above and added that between the two-monthly meetings of the All-Russian Central Executive Committee its powers would be exercised by a Praesidium. The dictatorship of the Party had commenced and the seeds sown for the dictatorship of the leader.

Courts

The new courts that were set up after the Revolution by the first Decree on the Courts, issued on 27 November 1917,[50] were not bound by the pre-1917 court system which was swept away, along with the legal profession. All Tsarist juridical structures were annihilated including the procuracy, the defence bar, investigating magistrates, justices of the peace and juries. When soldiers were sent to remove court personnel, the latter refused to recognize

---

50. *Sob. Uzak.* 1917. 4/50.

the government and its orders and went on strike.[51]
'Nothing like this,' says Richard Pipes, 'had ever happened
anywhere: Soviet Russia was the first state in history
formally to outlaw law.'[52] The only courts left were the
local courts (later known as People's Courts) which dealt
with minor crimes. By article 2 of the decree they were to
be nominated by the local Soviets, with a promise of
democratic elections sometime in the future. They were
composed of a president and two assessors with the latter
sitting for 10-day periods in a year over five years. The
assessors were selected by the executive committee of the
local Soviet from lists prepared by the workers'
organizations. These non-professional 'people's assessors',
who were to become a lasting feature of Soviet law in place
of the pre-existing juries introduced in the Judicial Reform
of 1864, were intended as a check on the president of the
court whom they could outvote on both questions of fact
and question of law and change any sentence he had in
mind. Whether they did so in practice is another matter
and they became contemptuously known as 'nodders'.

More ominously, by article 8 special revolutionary
tribunals, officially separate from the Cheka but to become
closely linked with it, had also been formed to try cases
involving counter-revolution and profiteering. In June
1918 the People's Commissar of Justice granted them
authority to pass death sentences. And, by article 5, laws

---

51. Samuel Kucherov. *The Organs of Soviet Administration of Justice: Their History and Operation.* (Leiden, E.J. Brill, 1970), pp.26-7.
52. *The Russian Revolution 1899-1919.* (London, Collins Harvill, 1990), p.796.

enacted before the Revolution were to be regarded as valid only in so far as they had not been abolished by the Revolution and did not contradict the 'revolutionary conscience and consciousness of justice'. The laws abolished, the article declared, were those which were contrary to Soviet decrees and those which contradicted the programmes of the Bolshevik and Left Socialist Revolutionary Parties. These programmes were henceforth to be treated as sources of law. (The Left Socialist Revolutionary Party was for a short time in uneasy alliance with the Bolsheviks in the Soviets as well as the Cheka and, when they could, they exercised a restraining influence.) The Tsarist code of punishments was replaced with punishments deemed to be required by the less certain 'circumstances of the case' and, again, by 'revolutionary consciousness'. At this stage detailed codes were not considered to be necessary since law would 'wither away'.

On 22 February 1918 the Central Executive Committee, over Lenin's signature, enacted a more precise law on the courts, known as the Second Decree.[53] This contained no reference to Party programmes and provided for district courts to try the more serious cases that were outside the competence of the local courts. By section 8, pre-existing laws on procedure were to be followed unless they contradicted 'the sense of justice of the toiling classes'. There were no restrictions on what evidence was to be admissible and, for civil cases, under section 36

---

53. *Sob. Uzak.* 1918. 26/420.

'considerations of justice, not of formal law, had to guide the decisions in satisfying evidently just claims, independently of prescription and other formal considerations'. In theory the people's assessors were now allowed to remove the president of the court at any stage of the proceedings.

By the Law on the People's Courts,[54] dated 30 November 1918, such courts were to be the only courts in Russia outside the revolutionary tribunals, and they were to hold three types of sessions:

1. The president sitting alone, for giving non-controversial decisions, granting divorce and ordering arrests.
2. The president sitting with two assessors, for the bulk of the civil and criminal cases. The assessors were to be chosen by lot and had to sit in six successive sessions of the court.
3. The president sitting with six assessors, for determining crimes against life, grievous bodily harm, rape, forgery, bribery and speculation in goods under state monopoly. In these latter cases the defence was entitled to counsel, but in less serious cases only if the court agreed. Capitalists and landlords were not eligible to be judges.

There was also to be a system of appeals but in the event appellate courts were not set up. However, by article 8 if

---

54. *Ibid.*, 1918/889.

the judge deviated from existing law on procedure on the ground that it was 'obsolete and bourgeois', he had to give his reasons so that a higher judicial body could check his interpretation of 'revolutionary consciousness'.

In February 1919, in line with the November decree the district courts were wound up and their functions were taken over by the people's courts, and by this time lawyers had been allowed back but as part of the salaried civil service. And a year later a department was established in the People's Commissariat of Justice to issue guiding instructions to the courts, to review their decisions and to declare a judgment void if considered contrary to the law, vague as it was, even if the decision had already been implemented.

As far as the revolutionary tribunals are concerned, by the decree of April 1919 they were given unlimited power to decide upon the required measure of repression, again based on the circumstances of the case and the demands of revolutionary consciousness. They were to be unhampered by any written law as there was to be no question of personal guilt, simply the defence of society. In fact, in the period 1920-1922 only one third of the persons in places of confinement were sentenced by ordinary courts. The others were convicted by the revolutionary tribunals or by the security police without resort to a court.[55]

---

55. Ger P. Van Den Berg. *The Soviet System of Justice: Figures and Policy.* (Dordrecht, Martinus Nijhoff Publishers, 1985), p.17.

Basic Principles

Apart from the courts, it was only on 12 December 1919 that the first systematic exposition of Soviet conceptions of law was provided in an administrative decree published by the People's Commissariat for Justice entitled, 'Basic Principles for the Criminal Law of the Soviet Republics'.[56] This was a general directive for lower courts and attempted to establish some kind of uniformity in punishment in order, it said, that workers might successfully deal with class enemies and teach themselves to rule. In part it read:

> Since the proletariat could not simply fit the going bourgeois state apparatus to its purposes but was required, having smashed it to fragments, to create its own state apparatus, likewise it could not fit to its purposes the bourgeois codes of the outlived epochs, which ought to have been placed in historical archives ... The experience of the struggle, however, has accustomed the proletariat to uniform measures, has led to a systematization, has given birth to new law. Almost two years of this struggle have already provided the opportunity to present the results as a concrete manifestation of proletarian law ...
>
> In the interest of conserving strength, of bringing isolated actions in conformity one with another, and of centralization, the proletariat must work out rules for

---

56. *Sob Uzak.* (1919). 66/590.

curbing its class enemies, for establishing a method in struggling with its enemies and must teach itself to rule. This relates first of all to criminal law, which has as its task the struggle with those who violate new rules for social intercourse, which have been developed during the transitional period of the dictatorship of the proletariat. Only when the opposition of the overthrown bourgeois and intermediate classes has been finally broken and where there exists a communist society, can the proletariat destroy the state as well, as an agency of persuasion, and law as a function of the state.

Article 5 declared that the criminal law defended the social structure of the existing society against violations (crimes) by repressive measures (penalties). Since there was no list of crimes and punishments it was for the judge to decide whether an act was dangerous to society and convict accordingly, and the class status of the offender was to be taken into account. Thus, it was important to distinguish an offence committed by a member of the property-owning class with the intention of creating or preserving social privileges from that of a destitute person in need or starving (art. 12). Furthermore, *potential future* acts of people with the wrong background were to be taken into account (author's italics). Thus, in the trial of two Catholic priests for treason in the spring of 1923, the state prosecutor, Nicolai Krylenko, demanded that the actions of accused individuals should be judged from the point of view of the 'social danger' they presented. In judging the criminal, he said, it was necessary to take into account 'not only what he has done, but what he may do in the future'.[57]

Penalties were meant to deter both the accused from further crime, and also potential criminals, in some cases by educational means or imprisonment, and, in others, by death. As crime was perceived to originate in the social structure of society article 10 specified that most punishments were not to inflict injurious and needless suffering – but this applied only to non-political offences such as theft. In general, for ordinary crimes there were maximum penalties not to be exceeded by the courts but for crimes against 'soviet order' there were minimum penalties which could not be reduced.

When, by 1921, the standards of War Communism were abandoned in favour of the New Economic Policy the tone had been set, particularly with the power of the political police and the concepts of 'revolutionary consciousness' and crimes determined by analogy. Indeed, as previously mentioned, what was established under Lenin's leadership in the period immediately after the Revolution laid the basis for Stalin's reign, involving both illegality and bloody terror behind a façade of law.

---

57. E.H. Carr. *A History of Soviet Russia: Socialism in One Country 1924-1926.* (Part Two), (London, Macmillan & Co., 1959), vol.6, p.434.

CHAPTER 2

Communist 'Legality'

Insurrection

The civil war and the brutal period of War Communism
left Russia in chaos and a state of collapse. Transport was
paralysed, industry virtually at a standstill, food and fuel
were in short supply and, following widespread seizures
of livestock, grain and seed by the government, an
appalling famine struck the countryside in which
uncounted millions died after agricultural production had
fallen by half. Many soldiers, workers and peasants who
had supported the Revolution to bring peace and order to
a war-stricken country now turned hostile to the
Bolsheviks. But Lenin was not about to seek allies or
relinquish power. As a result, in 1920-21 peasant risings,
some of them involving substantial numbers, occurred in
the main grain producing areas of the country and were
smashed by a terror which included the execution of whole
families as hostages and established another precedent for
Stalin later.

Perhaps the most well-known rising, amounting to an
insurrection, took place in Tambov, a relatively prosperous
agricultural province, 350 kilometres south-east of
Moscow. State requisitioning of grain and potatoes to feed

the army and the towns had reduced much of the rural population of Russia to starvation levels (not that the towns were much better off). As a consequence, many villages revolted and the Red Army went in burning them down and executing captured peasants. In response, Alexander Antonov, who had broken with the Bolsheviks over their agrarian policy, formed partisan units in Tambov of up to 50,000 farm workers and commenced a form of guerilla warfare. Among other things, he succeeded in cutting the railway lines, taking grain from the railway wagons and distributing it to hungry peasants. And over a large area he destroyed communist institutions and killed captured communists.

In return he and his followers were subjected to the unrestricted terror of the Cheka with executions of hostages and mass deportations to its labour camps. But they were finally defeated only by the massive force of 100,000 Red Army troops led by Tukhachevsky who, under a Party directive, proceeded to slaughter thousands of rebels and their families. Antonov himself was eventually captured and executed by the Cheka, but his guerilla methods were studied by the army and used effectively by partisans behind the German lines in the Second World War. And, once the peasants were subdued, in a preview of the New Economic Policy an anxious Lenin ordered the abolition of grain requisitioning in Tambov and had scarce supplies sent in from other districts.

This, and many other peasant risings, were followed by the Kronstadt sailors' revolt in 1921 that in its turn was crushed by 50,000 Red Army soldiers, again led by

Tukhachevsky who took care to have Cheka troops behind them during their attack on the Petersburg fortress during which over 10,000 soldiers met their death. Kronstadt had been in the forefront of the October Revolution and many of the rebels were Bolsheviks. But Lenin was quite prepared to suppress not only peasants but workers, sailors and anyone who fell out of line. It is significant therefore that the sailors complained that the régime had 'brought the workers, instead of freedom, an ever present fear of being dragged into the torture chambers of the Cheka, the horrors of which exceed by many times the rule of the gendarmerie administration of the Tsarist régime.'[1] As if to prove their point, over 2,500 of the rebels were shot without trial and many others were sent to the main concentration camp, a fifteenth-century monastery on the Solovetsky Islands in the White Sea.

One of the significant consequences of the revolutionary crisis in the country was the banning of factions within the Party which was later to be used by Stalin to divide and destroy Bolshevik opponents of his growing despotism. There is another point to be made here. Lenin not only turned on perceived 'renegades' like Karl Kautsky and former close friends like Yuli Martov but his own trusted colleagues in the Central Committee if they disagreed with him. His apparent forgiveness of Zinoviev and Kamenev for making public in advance the date of the October seizure of power was expedient and tactical. It is conjectural but from all we know of his conduct it is

---

1.   The sailors' *Izvestia*. 8 March 1921 in C.J. Scott. *Soviet Affairs*. I, p.14.

exceedingly plausible that had he lived longer he would have turned on Trotsky, Kamenev, Bukharin and the others as Stalin did.

The Impact of the New Economic Policy (1921-1928)

A retreat from War Communism and a temporary and partial restoration of capitalism became necessary if the economy, and the régime, were to survive. Accordingly, on Lenin's initiative, the New Economic Policy providing for a mixed economy was introduced by the Tenth Communist Party Congress in March 1921. The state retained control of heavy industry, foreign trade and banking but surrendered its monopoly of small-scale industrial establishments and retail trade and services. Money, which had been partially abolished under War Communism, was reintroduced into the economy. Market relations and private enterprise were encouraged and, in an attempt to appease the peasants, private rights in property were recognized and the surplus appropriation system in agriculture was replaced by a more lenient tax in kind. This latter measure left in the hands of peasants surpluses of produce which could be sold on the market.

But as it was considered that the NEP would involve to some extent a revival of petit bourgeois ideology, the centralization of the Party and its power was accelerated and its grip on the state machine was tightened, particularly when Stalin took control of a number of important bodies of the Party. Nevertheless, within the confines of a one-Party state, the NEP encouraged civil peace and economic recovery and in cultural and intellectual life some diversity and toleration were allowed to flourish for the time being.

Soviet Theory of Law

Although a number of decrees on law were necessarily issued during the period of War Communism, the general approach of Soviet jurists had been: 'Away with the Law.' That was now to change to: 'Return to the Law.' With the NEP a new attitude to legal policy came with a resolution of the Party Conference held in December 1921. This declared that, 'The immediate task is to introduce strict principles of revolutionary legality into all areas of life. The strict responsibility of governmental organs, governmental agents, and citizens for violating the laws of the soviet government and the order which it protects must be developed side by side with increased guarantees of the citizens' person and property.' [2]

This was a declaration that was to be continually breached by both Lenin and Stalin since the system of repression was above the law and decrees and penal codes often simply authorized the use of arbitrary power. Nevertheless, under the resolution more precise codes of criminal law, the mere idea of which had formerly been anathema as bourgeois relics, were to be introduced, the

---

2.   *Cf.* Zigurds L. Zile. (Madison, Wisconsin, 1970), 2nd edn, pp.66-7.

Procuracy was restored, lawyers encouraged and legal education resumed. All based on the supposition that law would be used to pave the way to its own eventual elimination.[3] As the ever-confident Bukharin put it in his influential *ABC of Communism*, 'As the state dies out, [the courts] will tend to become simply organs for the expression of public opinion. They will assume the character of courts of arbitration. Their decisions will no longer be enforced by physical means and they will have a purely moral significance.'[4]

Most Soviet legal theorists continued to consider that the law was a 'bourgeois fetish'. However, the distinguished jurist, Professor Hans Kelsen, says that 'The first important attempt to develop a specifically soviet theory of law – not as a mere by-product of a theory of the state – was P.L. Stuchka's *The Revolutionary Part Played by Law and the State: A General Doctrine of Law*, published in 1921.'[5]

Pavel Stuchka, the Commissar of Justice since late 1918, accepted the theory of Engels and Lenin that the law was determined by the forces of production and that after the Revolution criminal law would 'wither away' along with the need for political oppression, whilst civil law would go the same way once private enterprise was completely abolished. The proletariat, he said, in words

---

3. Introduction by Beirne and Sharlet to R. Conquest. *Justice and the Legal System in the USSR. Op. cit.*, p.15.
4. *Op. cit.*, p.226.
5. H. Kelsen. *The Communist Theory of Law.* (London, Stevens & Sons, 1955), p.62.

that he had inserted in the Basic Principles of Criminal Law in 1919, could not fit to its purposes the bourgeois codes of the outlived epochs, which ought to have been placed in historical archives.

'Communism,' he wrote, 'means not the victory of socialist law, but the victory of socialism over any law, since, with the abolition of classes with their economic interests, law will disappear altogether.'[6] In the meantime however, law would be useful as a means of coercion and he defined law as 'a system (or order) of social relations that corresponds to the interests of the dominant class and is safeguarded by the organized force of this class.' Criminal law, on the other hand, was 'composed of legal norms and other legal measures with which the system of social relationships of a given class society protects itself from violations (crimes) by means of repression (punishment).'[7]

Stuchka believed the 'most fundamental merit' of his definition of law was that, 'for the first time it puts upon firm scientific ground the problem of law in general: it renounces the purely formal [bourgeois] view of law and sees in law a changing social phenomenon rather than an eternal category. It renounces the attempt of bourgeois science to reconcile the irreconcilable, while on the contrary it finds a measure applicable to the most

6. P.L. Stuchka. *Encyclopaedia of State and Law.* (Moscow, State Publishing House, 1925-27), p.1593.
7. Stuchka. *The Revolutionary Part Played by Law and the State: A General Doctrine of Law.* In *Soviet Legal Philosophy.* (Moscow, State Publishing House, 1921), p.20.

irreconcilable species of law since it rests on the viewpoint of the class struggle and class contradictions.'[8] Here he seemed to be confusing the natural- law doctrine that perceives law as an eternal category with formalism which discounts social and moral content and he totally ignored the bourgeois sociological school which recognizes the historical and changing character of the law. Nevertheless, there was no confusion in his argument that, in line with Party policy, it was necessary for the 'coercive support of law' for the proletarian state 'to employ terror'.[9]

Trial of Left Socialist Revolutionaries

The month of June 1922 saw the trial, at Lenin's instigation, of his former allies, the popular leaders of the Left Socialist Revolutionary Party which had enjoyed a large majority of members in the ill-fated Constituent Assembly. They apparently staged an abortive coup, although Lenin was as averse to suffering allies as opponents and it may have resulted from a government provocation.[10] Indeed, Stalin had earlier taken the opportunity to send a telegram to the Central Executive Committee saying that the military council would respond to the criminal attempt on the life of Lenin with the organization of 'open, mass, systematic terror against the

---

8. *Ibid.,* p.20.
9. *Ibid.,* pp.67-69.
10. See Beryl Williams. *Lenin.* (Harlow, England, Longman, 2000), p.103.

bourgeoisie and its agents'.[11]

In what was the first show trial the accused were brought before the Supreme Revolutionary Tribunal charged with counter-revolutionary activities including treason and terrorism and, for good measure, organizing the nearly-blind Fanny Kaplan's shooting of Lenin in August 1918. In fact, apart from that attempted assassination in which they probably had no part, the acts alleged against them were made crimes only one week before the trial when they were in prison. As with Stalin's show trials in the 1930s a number of the 34 defendants, 13 of whom had been members of the Cheka, were made to incriminate not only themselves but the others as well, in particular the 12 members of the Left Socialist Revolutionary Central Committee who refused to co-operate in the trial.

All the judges were members of the Communist Party as was the prosecutor, Nicolai Krylenko. Many witnesses for the defence were not allowed to testify and four eminent defence lawyers who arrived from abroad soon refused to proceed in what they called a 'parody of justice'. When a crowd was allowed to enter the courtroom shouting 'Death to the Murderers!' Bukharin said they were expressing the 'voice of the workers', a patently false claim that was to haunt him in his own frame-up of a trial in 1938. All the defendants were found guilty and, despite earlier promises to the contrary, 14 were sentenced to death, whilst those who had assisted the prosecution

---

11. *Collected Works.* (Moscow, State Publishing House), vol.vi, p.128.

received pardons. Eighteen months later, after they had agreed to abandon the struggle against Soviet power, those sentenced to death had the penalty commuted to five years' imprisonment. No such 'leniency' was to be exhibited again and, indeed, the Left Socialist Revolutionary Party was banned and hundreds of its members imprisoned or killed.

Criminal Codes

The first criminal code of the Russian Federation (RSFSR) was enacted in May 1922[12] and was quickly adopted by the other Soviet republics. In the main it brought together earlier individual decrees and directives and article 6 defined crime not as a breach of law but as 'any socially dangerous act or omission ... threatening the foundation of soviet authority and legal order established by the worker-peasant power for the time of transition to a communist system.' And, by article 7, 'The danger of a person is shown by the commission of acts harmful to society, or if his activities exhibit a grave threat to the social legal order.' Lenin, who was involved in drawing up the Code, insisted to Commissar of Justice Kritsky that the death sentence should be extended to cover anti-soviet agitation, propaganda and activity by Mensheviks and Socialist Revolutionaries. Thus did state power and the criminal law coalesce with intent more important than an act or deed. It was hardly likely to be otherwise when

---

12. *Sob. Uzak.* 1922/153.

prosecutor Nicolai Krylenko, hero of the civil war and later to be People's Commissar of Justice, wrote in 1923, 'We look at the court as a class institution, as an organ of government power, and we erect it as an organ completely under the control of the vanguard of the working class (i.e., the Party). Our judge is above all a politician, a worker in the political field. A club is a primitive weapon, a rifle is a more efficient one, the most efficient is the court.'[13]

At least article 26 declared that punishment must be 'expedient, and at the same time completely free of signs of torture and must not cause useless and unnecessary suffering to the criminal.' A provision that, alas, was to be more recognized in the breach than the observance, although for non-political crimes such as hooliganism and home brewing non-custodial sanctions were widely used.

The Procuracy

In the same month of May 1922 a decree[14] established the office of Public Procurator (investigator and prosecutor). He was in theory to be subject only to the Supreme Court, which was itself subject to the Central Executive Committee, but he became an important figure in Soviet law on behalf of Stalin. To Lenin the procuracy was intended to centralize legal authority. It was indeed a

---

13. Quoted in Harold J. Berman. *Justice in the USSR: An Interpretation of Soviet Law.* (Cambridge, Mass. Harvard University Press, 1963), p.36.
14. *Sov. Uzak.* 1922/424.

highly centralized institution and the procurators' functions, although not their name, were unique to the Soviet Union. They were also intended by Lenin in 1922 not only to prosecute criminals but also to control the revolutionary zeal of the Soviets during the partial restoration of capitalism under the New Economic Policy.

In the official language they were to prosecute persons accused of violating the law, supervise the legality of the actions of all bodies exercising public authority and complain to the Supreme Court if they considered that decisions were too harsh or too lenient. More will be heard of them later, particularly after Vyshinsky took over the leading role and, following Krylenko, declared that any conflicts between the requirements of the law and the commands of the Revolution 'must be solved only by the subordination of the formal commands of law to those of Party policy.'[15]

In the meantime, Party directives gave the political objectives that determined how the Procuracy should operate and, in the main, both the Procuracy and the courts were staffed by Party members. Not that this was always sufficient. The Smolensk archives (of which more in chapter 5) set out the assessments made of some people's judges. For example, in a memorandum of the District Party Control Commission of 20 August 1928 we find:

---

15. Andrei Y. Vyshinsky. *The Judicial System of the USSR*. (Moscow, State Publishing House, 1936), p.24.

I.F. Fedorovich:
– (a judge of a district court) is a peasant from Smolensk ... 40 years old. Member of the CPSU(B). Five years, five months in the organs of justice. Has no legal education, General education – intermediate. In a local court since the end of 1926. He manages the apparatus of justice poorly. Is afraid of the officials. *Can fall under the influence of the legal line* (author's italics), does not hold to class and punitive policy well enough ...

S.A. Akimov:
– people's judge, city of Sychevka –
Akimov is a local peasant, member of the CPSU(B), 30 years old, in the organs of justice for two years, five months. Education – lower. Before he was in the organs of justice he worked in lower Party and co-operative work. Illiterate in legal matters. Because of insufficient supervision and guidance in the cases examined he does not at all hold to the class line, especially when he is at meetings of the land commission. Many of his sentences are confused and have no basis ...[16]

Other similar assessments followed and it is difficult to understand how these largely uneducated Party members were elected or appointed judges other than because of such membership. But even that was not enough if they deviated from the class line.

---

16. Merle Fainsod. *Smolensk under Soviet Rule*. (London, Macmillan & Co., 1958), p.178.

Bearing in mind Stalin's theory of the 'intensification of the class struggle under socialism' it is worthy of note that in 1934 one procurator in the Smolensk region reported that he had discovered no anti-Soviet groups, that he considered the political situation to be 'fully satisfactory' and that the attitude of the population towards Soviet authority was 'quite loyal' except for 'insignificant strata'. Another procurator in the region had reported similarly in 1926.[17]

The OGPU is Born

As we have seen, once the New Economic Policy was introduced the Party set about trying to achieve internal stability and legal legitimacy but still within the context of 'revolutionary legality'. As a result, in a largely cosmetic change, in February 1922 the Cheka was abolished and replaced by the GPU (State Political Administration), but retained the Cheka's administrative powers, although it was placed under the NKVD (Commissariat for Internal Affairs).[18] Whereas the Cheka had in the main sought enemies outside the Party, the GPU was now to look for them inside the Party as well. Then, as part of the Constitution of the USSR ratified in January 1924, the GPU in turn, by a decree dated 15 November 1923,[19] was

---

17. *Ibid.*, pp.174-6.
18. *Sob. Uzak.* 1922. 16/160.
19. *Ibid.* 1924. 12/105.

replaced by the OGPU (Unified State Political Administration), which was given all-union functions and was not subject to the NKVD.

Instead, it was attached to the Council of People's Commissars but it retained as its head the old Cheka chief, Felix Dzerzhinsky. It was authorized to recruit its own troops and border guards and take over the militia and it held a monopoly of police functions until 1934. It also controlled a vast network of spies and informers in factories, government offices, units of the Red Army and the forced-labour camps. Informing was actively promoted, even against members of one's own family, not only as a patriotic duty but also as a service to the person denounced and conducive to the well-being of society. The OGPU was permitted to impose the death penalty for sabotage, arson, destruction of state property and wrecking, and to banish to forced-labour camps for three years, persons who had been convicted at least twice for certain crimes, and members of 'anti-soviet parties'. How many prisoners this involved is indicated by the rise in the number of forced-labour camps from 84 in 1920 to 315 in October 1923.[20]

With the advent of the OGPU as a permanent political police under the Constitution, and largely an administrative organ free of control by the courts, the revolutionary tribunals were abolished and their formal functions transferred to Gubernia (regional) Courts,

---

20. Richard Pipes. *Russia Under the Bolshevik Regime: 1919-1924.* (London, Harvill, 1994), p.400.

themselves subject to the Supreme Courts of the union republics and, above them, the Supreme Court of the USSR. They had the power to impose the death penalty for a number of crimes including serious cases of bribery, the passing of unjust sentences by judges for reasons of personal interest, aggravated robbery and misuse of official power (arts.110-130). However, they soon assumed even greater and more wide-ranging punitive powers, although the secret police remained the main agency for enforcing terror.

Creation of the USSR

In the new situation under the New Economic Policy, on 30 December 1922 the Soviet republics of Russia, the Ukraine, Belorussia and Transcaucasia (after its Menshevik government was overthrown by force) were combined to form the Union of Soviet Socialist Republics (USSR). Out of the window now went the right of nations to self-determination which had earlier been espoused by Stalin in his *Marxism and the National and Colonial Question* in 1913.[21] As Leszek Kolakowski has expressed it in his *Main Currents of Marxism*, 'Separatist movements are progressive when directed against bourgeois governments, but once the "proletariat" is in power national separatism automatically and dialectically changes its significance, since it is a threat to the

---

21. (London, Lawrence & Wishart Ltd., 1942).

proletarian state, socialism and world revolution.'[22]

Just over a year later, on 31 January 1924 the USSR, adopted its first Constitution and, anticipating the Cominform in 1948, made the first declaration that the world was divided into two camps – the capitalist and the socialist. Supreme power was vested in the Party-controlled Congress of Soviets, which was hardly to be taken seriously since it was to meet for only one short period each year. Between its meetings its place was taken by the Central Executive Committee which it elected, as before. When that was not in session, and it met only infrequently, its Praesidium (the real Party power) had full legislative, executive and administrative powers and appointed the members of the Council of People's Commissars, ostensibly the government. This problem of the government being subservient to the Party was of course the cause of so many ills of the Soviet Union throughout its existence.

The first All-Union Supreme Court was established, according to article 43 of the Constitution, 'in order to maintain revolutionary legality[23] but it was made subordinate to the Central Executive Committee and the Party which effectively retained judicial power. New criminal codes were adopted by republics across the whole of the Soviet Union by 1926. In general, the government issued fundamental principles of law to be observed throughout the land and these were adapted into the codes

---

22. (Oxford, Clarendon Press, 1978), vol.iii, p.14.
23. Zigurds. *Op. cit.,* p.72.

by the union republics.

To some extent the provisions of earlier codes were reintroduced. Again, every act or omission directed against the régime was to be treated as a crime and counter-revolutionary activities and *intentions* were to be dealt with severely. Furthermore, the doctrine of analogy, which by-passes the principle of law that there can be no penalty except for a violation of a specific legal provision, was explicitly reintroduced from the earlier codes. By article 16 of the RSFSR 1926 criminal code, 'If any socially dangerous act is not directly provided for by the present code, the basis and extent of liability for it is determined by application of those articles of the code which deal with the offences most similar to it in nature.'[24] In other words if a person could not under the law be convicted for adultery he could be convicted of theft. The concept of analogy was not eliminated from the criminal law until December 1958.

Shortly after the adoption of the RSFSR criminal code a new all-union law on counter-revolutionary crimes was enacted and incorporated into the 1926 code on 6 June 1927 – the infamous article 58, of which more will be said later. As non-political crimes, including rape, theft, robbery and the infliction of bodily harm, were believed to be the product of social conditions their perpetrators were to be subject to corrective measures. These were often severe enough but not as brutal as the punishments meted

---

24. *Sob. Zak. (Collections of Laws and Regulations of the USSR.* In Official Gazette 1924-28). 1926. 80/600.

out under article 58. At the same time the OGPU had extensive powers to banish without trial even where counter-revolutionary activities were merely *suspected* (author's italics). Indeed, in 1928 the eighteenth plenum of the Supreme Court introduced the conception of 'eventual intention' into the definition of counter-revolutionary sabotage under the soon to be added article 58(7) of the code.[25] It is significant that official figures for the number of penalties (including fines) in the year 1928, 11 years after the 'workers revolution', amounted to four and a half million.[26]

25. Schlesinger. *Op. cit.,* p.209.
26. Van Den Berg. *Op. cit.,* p.13.

CHAPTER 3

Stalin in Power

The First Five-Year-Plan

What is known as the Second Revolution, called by Stalin himself the 'Revolution from above', was heralded in 1928. This war against the nation involved abandonment of the New Economic Policy, which Stalin had previously supported but now saw as 'rotten liberalism', and introduced a totally different kind of society from that envisaged in the October Revolution with its initial emphasis on mass participation. In effect it was more decisive in changing the country than the October Revolution or the purges and was supported by workers who had suffered from unemployment under the NEP which they saw as a pro-peasant and anti-working class policy. The aim of the Plan was no less than to revitalize the country by central planning with the OGPU in control of the economy.

Lagging industrial production, low grain deliveries, distrust among Party members about where the NEP was leading and fear of foreign intervention were the motives for Stalin's change of course. The NEP's replacement was the First Five-Year-Plan under which heavy industry was to be expanded in a crash programme by the use of modern technology and a vast low-skilled labour force, including slave labour. It was given priority over plants producing consumer goods. The fixed capital stock of industry was projected to double with enormous increases in the production of iron and coal. Labour productivity was set to rise by 110 per cent and agricultural production by 55 per cent. Stalin was now adopting the previously anathema policy of his former opponents but consistency was never his forte and a similar situation was to occur when he decided upon the collectivization in agriculture.

Not surprisingly, attempts in industry to achieve impossible targets resulted in bottlenecks, confusion and shortages. As a result, many of the predictions of the Plan were not fulfilled but heavy industry and military supplies were transformed, although at great cost in material and loss of life. Classes in society, it was now claimed, would disappear by 1937 when the law would be replaced by planning: the transformation from the 'government of persons' by the 'administration of things' forecast by Engels.[1]

The Theory of Law in Flux

The law codes promulgated under the NEP were still considered not to have embodied a new socialist system of law but were regarded as laws of a transition period

---

1. Engels. *Socialism: Utopian and Scientific.* In *Marx and Engels Selected Works. Op. cit.*, vol.ii, p.138.

during which they would wither away. The pre-eminent Marxist legal theorist by this time was E.B. Pashukanis who held that the origin of law lay in the market-place and laws reflected commodity exchange, although this could hardly apply to criminal law. There was, he said, no such thing as proletarian law and such law as existed was simply bourgeois law with an economic basis founded upon commodity exchange and could not be given a socialist content. Even in criminal law, he said, the principle of retribution was the mere expression of the narrow views of the commodity dealer who claimed equal and just compensation if his goods had been destroyed. He believed criminal codes should omit any mention of specific crimes and punishments and should allow judges to apply general principles to individual cases as well as using the principle of analogy. Accordingly, when the capitalist system of commodity exchange came to be finally abolished under socialism all law would disappear along with the state which, like classes, he forecast would wither away by the end of the Second Five-Year-Plan in 1937.

When D.N. Pritt, KC, visited the Soviet Union in the early 1930s he was told in the Commissariat of Justice that all civil and criminal litigation would disappear within the next six or seven years, and that those who disagreed with such a prediction found it only 'much too short'.[2] However, such thinking by Pashukanis and other jurists was becoming dangerous since by this time Stalin

---

2.   D.N. Pritt. 'The Russian Legal System'. In *Twelve Studies in Soviet Russia*. Ed. Margaret I. Cole. (London, Victor Gollancz Ltd., 1933), p.165.

was building a centralized, bureaucratic, state power from above and needed to continue using and reinforcing the law as one of the coercive instruments of that power.

New laws which were introduced around this time included one of 1929[3] which made officials who defected, or who had previously defected, subject to capital punishment, and another in the same year[4] established new labour camps in remote regions as general places of imprisonment. And in 1930, a law changed the minimum term of imprisonment from one day to one year.[5] So 'sacred' was state-owned property regarded that in that year when two young men broke a window in a clinic they had to admit intent to harm the Soviet state. However, in this case the Russian Supreme Court did reclassify their action from counter-revolutionary destruction of state property to the less serious crime of wilful destruction of property belonging to state institutions.[6] Generally, if the accused had a bourgeois background criminal intent would be assumed, and was often difficult to disprove. It should also be noted that decisions of the Supreme Court, although treated with respect by lower courts, lacked the binding force of precedent, a concept which was not accepted in the Soviet Union.

A repressive law was passed on 7 August 1932 under the clumsy title of 'Law on Protection of Property of State Enterprises, Collective Farms and Co-operatives and on

---

3. *Sob. Zak.* (1929). 76/732.
4. *Ibid.* (1929). 72/686.
5. *Ibid.* (1930). 9/51.
6. Quoted by Hazard. *Op. cit.*, p.97.

the Strengthening of Social (Socialist) Ownership.'[7] The types of property mentioned in the decree, including livestock and even small quantities of crops such as a few ears of corn, were held to be sacred and inviolable and persons breaking this law by theft were to be treated as enemies of the people with death or deportation to a labour camp the penalty. On 8 June 1934 the decree was amended to 'Law on Crimes Against the State.'[8] This was a less awkward title but its provisions were even more repressive and wide-ranging. Added to article 58 of the RSFSR criminal code it also provided for a new offence of treason known as 'Betrayal of the Motherland,' which covered a multitude of activities, and even words.

Intensification of the Class Struggle under Socialism

In 1925 Nikolai Ivanovich Bukharin, a member of the Politburo, soon to be leader of the Comintern and an intellectual whom Lenin in his Testament described as 'the greatest and most valuable theoretician' and 'the favourite of the whole Party,'[9] had published a pamphlet entitled *The Path to Socialism and the Worker-Peasant Alliance.*[10]

---

7. *Sob. Zak.* (1932). 62/360.
8. *Ibid.* (1934). 33/255.
9. Isaac Deutscher. *Stalin: A Political Biography.* (London, Penguin Books, 1966), p.252.
10. Sidney Heitman, ed. *Nicolai I. Bukharin: A Bibliography.* (Stanford, California, The Hoover Institute on War, Revolution and Peace. Stanford University, 1967).

In it he wrote:

> When, for instance, kulaks,[11] or people who are growing rich at the expense of others and have crept into the organs of the Soviet government, begin to shoot village correspondents, it is a manifestation of the class struggle in its most acute form. However, such incidents, as a rule, occur in those places where the local Soviet apparatus is weak. As this apparatus improves, as all the lower units of the Soviet government become stronger, as the local, village Party and Young Communist League organizations improve and become stronger, such phenomena, it is perfectly obvious, will become more and more rare and will finally disappear leaving no trace.

Here it might be thought that Bukharin was merely expressing a Marxist truth following Engels' theory that the oppressive state machine would wither away. Whilst accepting the reality of the class struggle Bukharin had always defended the NEP as allowing a gradual development towards socialism. And in 1925 he also called for a renewal of the independent role of the Soviets, an emphasis on the rule of law and professional planning of the economy. In contrast Zinoviev and Kamenev were advocating more intensified industrialization as well as opposition to Stalin's leadership. As a consequence, Stalin formed an alliance with Bukharin in favour of continuing

---

11. Russian for 'fist'. Usually a well-to-do peasant.

the NEP and against Zinoviev and Kamenev. By December 1927 the Fifteenth Party Congress, after refusing to allow Trotsky, Zinoviev and Kamenev to speak, had approved their expulsion from the Party together with a number of their leading supporters who were to be executed in the Great Terror in the Thirties.

But when, in 1928 and 1929, Stalin himself embarked on a programme of vast schemes for a super heavy industry to be paid for by a form of colonial 'tribute' from the peasantry, Bukharin joined with Alexei Rykov, chairman of the Council of People's Commissars, and Mikhail Tomsky, leader of the Soviet trade unions, in opposition to Stalin and this was eventually to lead to his execution 10 years later. Bukharin had accepted, even originated, the concept of socialism in one country but was opposed to Stalin's abuses of power and in place of plans for forced industrialization and collectivization he argued instead for less hasty measures in industry and agriculture, and proposed conciliatory policies with a slow growth to socialism based on Soviet law. However, by this time Stalin had pronounced his new theory that as society progressed towards socialism instead of the class struggle diminishing it actually intensified.

In August 1928 Bukharin met Kamenev (now back in the Party after having recanted his errors and denounced Trotskyism), in an attempt to secure an alliance against what he called Stalin's 'illiterate and illogical' idea that the further socialism advanced, the stronger would popular resistance to it become, a resistance that only 'firm leadership' could hold down. 'This means a police state,' said Bukharin, but 'Stalin will stop at nothing, his policy is leading us to civil war; he will be compelled to drown rebellions in blood ... The root of the evil is that Party and state are so completely merged. He will slay us. He is the new Genghiz Khan.'[12] Bukharin asked Kamenev to keep their meeting a secret but the latter sent a detailed account to Zinoviev from whom it passed to followers of Trotsky abroad who published details of it which inevitably reached the ears of Stalin. No doubt they were happy to exacerbate the tensions within the Soviet leadership.

On the theory of the intensification of the class struggle Bukharin told a joint plenum of the Central Committee and the Central Control Commission, the Party's tyrannical disciplinary body, in April 1929:

This peculiar theory takes the bare fact that an intensification of the class struggle is now taking place and elevates it into some sort of inevitable law of our development. According to this strange theory, it would seem that the further we advance towards socialism, the more difficulties will pile up and the sharper the class struggle will become, and at the very gates to socialism we apparently will either have to start a civil war or, perishing from hunger, lay down our bones to die.[13]

---

12. Isaac Deutscher. *The Prophet Unarmed: Trotsky 1921-1929*. (London, Oxford University Press, 1959), pp.441-2.
13. Quoted by Roy Medvedev. *Let History Judge: The Origins and Consequences of Stalinism*. (New York, Columbia University Press, 1989), p.202.

Attack on Bukharin

In view of Stalin's revisions of Marxism and his changes on policy towards industry and the peasantry this was throwing down the gauntlet with a vengeance. Stalin responded by deciding to confront and undermine Bukharin and his gradualist approach (which Stalin had previously accepted) in a speech on 'The Right Deviation in the CPSU(B)' at the same meeting in the second half of April 1929. By this time, having defeated his potential rivals, Trotsky, Zinoviev and Kamenev, Stalin had introduced more of his supporters into the top echelons of the Party including the Politburo and the Central Committee, and assumed supreme power. He now made a savage attack on Bukharin's 'right deviation', alleging that his theory of the state was anti-Leninist and that he wallowed in a 'semi-anarchistic puddle'.[14] We were now, he continued, in the period of reconstruction of the national economy on the basis of socialism. And, with an ominous reaffirmation, 'This new period gives rise to new class changes, to an intensification of the class struggle.'

Bukharin, however, declared Stalin, had said 'Can our kulak really be called a kulak? Why, he is a pauper. And our middle peasant, is he really like a middle peasant? Why, he is a pauper, leading a half-starved existence.' Such a conception of the peasantry, said Stalin, was incompatible with Leninism which saw the peasantry as

---

14. J. Stalin. *Problems of Leninism.* (Moscow, Foreign Languages Publishing House, 1947), pp.238-88.

the last capitalist class.[15] How that would refute
Bukharin's statements about the poverty of kulaks and
middle peasants he did not explain. Presumably capitalists
could not be paupers. In any event, at the Eighth Moscow
Trade Union Congress in 1927 Bukharin himself had
stated:

> The implementation of the line of the Fourteenth
> Conference and Fourteenth Congress reinforced the
> alliance with the middle peasant and strengthened the
> proletariat's position in the countryside. Now together
> with the middle peasant, and relying on the poor
> peasant and on the growing economic and political
> forces of our Union and Party, it is possible and
> necessary to make a transition to an accelerated
> offensive against the capitalist elements, primarily the
> kulaks.[16]

He was often praised in the Party for speaking his mind
and admitting his mistakes and if he had changed his
mind since 1927 so had Stalin, who had often supported
Bukharin's policies in the past.

Stalin now further reproached Bukharin for his
'blindness' and non-Marxist approach in not seeing that
Stalin's perceived intensification of the class struggle was
taking place in industry and agriculture. Admitting that
the 'dying classes' were growing weaker under socialism,

---

15. *Ibid.*
16. *Pravda.* 13 October 1927.

he nevertheless claimed that their resistance was growing stronger. This new 'theory' was to lead to the trials of so-called wreckers in industry and the horrors involved in the liquidation of the kulaks as a class.

But first he had to 'liquidate' Bukharin as a Marxist. 'Of course,' he said, 'Bukharin is a theoretician of no mean calibre.' But he had piled up a heap of mistakes on Comintern questions, on questions of the class struggle, on the peasantry and on the New Economic Policy. Hence, he was not altogether a Marxist theoretician. Lenin, averred Stalin, had said Bukharin had never fully understood dialectics.[17] This was quite something coming from Stalin who had found it necessary to take lessons in dialectics from the leading philosopher Jan Sten from 1925 to 1928 until he claimed to be able to point out errors in the philosophy of G.V. Plekhanov, widely regarded as the 'Father of Russian Marxism.'[18]

In the event, Bukharin was soon removed from his post as leader of the Comintern and expelled from the Politburo and his editorship of *Pravda*. Later, alongside millions of others, including Jan Sten and other philosophers, he was executed during the bloody purges of the Terror. It might be said that Stalin was sensibly updating Marxism in new conditions but, of course, it was he who was intensifying, in the name of the class struggle, his battle against millions of imaginary 'enemies of the people', including

---

17. Stalin. *Problems of Leninism. Op. cit.*
18. Robert C. Tucker. *Stalin in Power: The Revolution from Above 1928-1941.* (New York, W.W. Norton and Company, 1990), pp.149-50.

people', including many trusted communists.

Giving his report to the Sixteenth Party Congress in June and July 1930, a year after his speech to the Central Committee, Stalin said in relation to the intensification of the class struggle and the building of socialism in one country:

It may be said that such a way of approaching the question is 'contradictory'. But is there not the same 'contradiction' in our treatment of the question of the state? We are in favour of the dying-away of the state, and at the same time we stand for the strengthening of the dictatorship of the proletariat, which represents the most powerful and mighty authority of all forms of which have existed up to the present day. The highest possible development of the power of the state, with the object of preparing the conditions for the dying away of the state: that is the Marxist formula. Is it 'contradictory'? Yes, it is 'contradictory'. But this contradiction is a living thing, and completely reflects Marxist dialectics.[19]

In reality, Stalin's slogan put a new gloss on Marxism and the theory of Lenin. Marx considered that there could be no socialism until the state had withered away. Without referring to the state in this context, in 1915 Lenin had written that, 'the unevenness of political and economic

---

19. Stalin. *Political Report to the Sixteenth Party Congress of the Russian Communist Party.* (London, Modern Books Limited, 1930), pp.171-72.

development is an unconditional law of capitalism. Hence it follows that the victory of socialism is possible in the *first instance* in a few capitalist countries or even in one single capitalist country.'[20] Stalin construed this to show that Lenin had considered socialism in one country to be possible. But as E.H Carr, in his voluminous study of early Soviet Russia has pointed out the passage related primarily to the seizure of power, not the building of a socialist economy: nor could it be shown that Lenin had Russia in mind at all.[21]

Pashukanis, quoting Stalin profusely, now debased himself in a report to the bureau of the Institute of Soviet Construction and Law on 10 November 1930 under the title *The Soviet State and the Revolution in Law*.[22] He admitted to having been influenced by Bukharin and having himself been in error in advancing theoretical propositions about the state and the law based on Bukharin's false formulations, particularly the idea that the state gives a unity to society. He had, he said, muddled Engels' work on the origins of the state, but he would not accept as the function of criminal law what he called the 'left-deviation' that 'all our repression be organized as terror'. He confirmed that he stood by the general content of his book, *Law and Marxism: A General Theory*, which had been published in 1925.[23] And for the time being he

20. Quoted by Carr. *A History of Soviet Russia: Socialism in One Country 1924-1926.* (London, Macmillan, 1959), vol.vi, pp.40-41.
21. *Ibid.*, p.41.
22. Babb. *Soviet Legal Theory. Op. cit.*, pp.237-80.
23. Pashukanis (ed. C. Arthur, trans. B. Einholm, Ink Links, London, 1978).

survived, although the 'left-deviation' he mentioned would destroy him when adopted by Vyshinsky.

Trials in Industry

As part of his strategy to end the New Economic Policy and justify his theme of the intensification of the class struggle, Stalin had earlier decided to attack 'bourgeois specialists' in industry with a series of public trials in Moscow. The first, lasting from 18 May to 15 July 1928, was the Shakhty case from the coal-mining region of the Donbas and it represented the beginning of the Terror. Fifty-three engineers and technicians, including three from Germany, were described as 'class enemies' and accused of wrecking equipment, causing accidents and having contact with the former capitalist owners of the mines. After being held by the OGPU for almost a year, 10 of the prisoners made full confessions and six others partial ones. These constituted the only evidence before the court. Two attempts to recant in court failed under pressure from the prosecutor, one by the accused Skorutto, whose wife had cried out in court, 'Kolya, darling, don't lie. Don't! You know you are innocent,' being particularly harrowing.

The case was tried before a Special Assize of the Supreme Court in the vast Hall of Columns in Moscow with Andrei Y. Vyshinsky as the presiding judge. The state prosecutor was Nicolai V. Krylenko who was chief prosecutor for many years and later People's Commissar of Justice before finally being shot as a traitor in 1940. No doubt accidents and damage to foreign machinery for which there were no spare parts had occurred, and many of the workers had only recently come from the farms and were inexperienced. However, to illustrate the Soviet concepts of 'legality' and a fair trial, the Party and the press whipped up a campaign of 'death to the wreckers' and at the end of the trial 11 death sentences were passed and five experts were executed. These were early days for such trials and two Soviet lawyers acting for the Germans dared to say that their clients were innocent. They were immediately arrested in the courtroom and taken away by the secret police.[24]

Stalin used the trial to discredit Bukharin's policy of working with non-Bolshevik specialists and Tomsky's leadership of the trade unions as part of his 'intensification of the class struggle' thesis. Furthermore, he immediately told what may have been a bemused Central Committee of the Party that the affair was part of an economic counter-revolution and that every branch of Soviet industry was filled with wreckers who made up one of the most dangerous forms of opposition to developing socialism.[25] In the resulting witch-hunt thousands of loyal engineers were dismissed or arrested and tried. The most famous was Pyotr Palchinsky who had been persecuted under the Tsar for revolutionary activity and after the February Revolution of 1917 was appointed Deputy

---

24. *The Times.* 12 April 1933.
25. Stalin. *Collected Works.* (London, Lawrence & Wishart Ltd. 1954), vol.xi, p.57.

Minister of Trade and Industry. From 1920 he had been a professor at the Mining Institute and a consultant to Gosplan (the State Planning Commission). An unlikely saboteur, he was accused of heading a nationwide engineers' organization of wreckers. Although tortured by OGPU interrogators he refused to plead guilty or sign a confession and is believed to have been killed during their interrogation of him.

In 1930 a new counter-revolutionary organization was 'uncovered', the so-called Toiling Peasant Party. Alleged leaders and members were arrested and tried in a closed court. They were found guilty and shot, only to be rehabilitated in 1987 when the Supreme Court declared that the 'Toiling Peasant Party' had never existed. This case was followed by the public trial of the 'Industrial Party' (Prompartiya) the aims of which were said to be to organize sabotage and espionage and prepare for the intervention of the Western powers and the overthrow of the Soviet government. The eight defendants, including the prominent engineer Professor Ramzin, confessed and were sentenced to various terms of imprisonment. The fact that they were not sentenced to death may have something to do with the flimsy nature of the evidence against them (there was no documentary evidence and the only witnesses were prisoners) and the fact that foreign correspondents were allowed to be in court. But, in any event, it had served another purpose in that the net of the terror was now spreading far wider than the trials themselves. Sidney and Beatrice Webb who were friendly to the Soviet Union and generally saw it through rose-coloured spectacles, nevertheless wrote of the Industrial Party trial:

This much-discussed prosecution of Professor Ramzin and his colleagues inaugurated a veritable reign of terror against the intelligentsia. Nobody regarded himself as beyond suspicion. Men and women lived in daily dread of arrest. Thousands were sent on administrative exile to distant parts of the country. Evidence was not necessary. The title of engineer served as sufficient condemnation. The jails were filled. Factories languished from lack of technical leadership, and the chiefs of the Supreme Economic Council commenced to complain 'that by its wholesale arrests of engineers the GPU ... was interfering with industrial progress.'[26]

Trials in other sectors of the economy followed. Forty-eight senior officials of the food industry were charged with sabotaging food supplies, especially in the meat, fish and vegetable agencies, and causing famine in various parts of the country. In a secret trial all 48 were sentenced to be shot.

March 1931 saw the public 'Menshevik Trial' in which economic specialists in Gosplan itself were accused of criminal activity in attempting to undermine industrial growth by proposing low planning targets and engaging

---

26. *Soviet Communism: A New Civilization?* (London, Longman, 1936), vol.ii, p.553.

in espionage. An important part in the trial was played with the allegation that one of the Menshevik leaders in exile, Raphael Abramovitch, had entered the Soviet Union illegally. In fact, at the time he was attending a Congress of the Socialist International as numerous witnesses confirmed. On the other hand, two Mensheviks who had entered the country illegally were not produced at the trial. After confessing their guilt the accused were sentenced to terms of imprisonment.[27]

And on 12 April 1933, six employees of the giant British engineering combine, Metro-Vickers, who were working in the Soviet Union under a technical aid agreement, were arrested with a number of Russians. They were charged before the Supreme Court under article 58 with military and economic espionage, wrecking machinery in power stations and concealing organic defects in machinery supplied by Metro-Vickers. V.V. Ulrich was the presiding judge and Andrei Y. Vyshinsky the chief prosecutor.[28] No British counsel was allowed to represent them or be present in court. The Britons had been working in Russia for some years without trouble. One of them, Leslie Thornton, together with the Russians, pleaded guilty and the remaining Britons pleaded not guilty. Thornton's detailed admissions, extracted, he said, 'under great pressure', involved some of the other British defendants

---

27. Details of these trials and some of those accused can be found in Roy Medvedev. *Let History Judge.* (New York, Columbia University Press, 1989), pp.258-84.
28. Verbatim Report: *Wrecking Activities at Power Stations in the Soviet Union.* (London, George Allen & Unwin, 1933), pp.1-798.

and virtually destroyed any chance they might have had of acquittal. They also complained about the evidence against them being given by 'terrorized' Russian prisoners. The fact that a year later the Soviet Union was again using Metro-Vickers engineers indicates that the trial was directed at intimidating Russian workers.

Reporters from the British press were present and Vyshinsky took the opportunity to make a lengthy attack on the English judicial system. At the end of the trial one of the British defendants was acquitted, Thornton was given a three year prison sentence and another, Macdonald, two years. The remainder were deported. One Russian was released and eight were given various sentences of imprisonment. No legal appeal was allowed but according to the British Foreign Secretary, Sir John Simon, replying to a question in the House of Commons, Thornton and Macdonald were told they could apply for commutation to the Central Executive Committee.[29] The trial caused a storm in Britain where the government broke off trade relations with the Soviet Union and D.N. Pritt, KC, launched the first of his eulogies of Soviet justice and courts.[30]

The Times was well-informed about Soviet legality and in its leader on 12 April it claimed that the 'trial' was framed to find scapegoats for breakdowns in Soviet industry through mismanagement and lack of skilled

---

29. *Hansard* [277] Fifth Series, cols.19-20.
30. W.P. Coates. *The Moscow Trial* (April 1933). With a Preface by Pritt. (London, The Anglo-Russian Parliamentary Committee, 1933), p.9.

workers. It was it said a 'tragic farce' with incredible charges based on manufactured evidence and fantastic confessions. The appearance of the accused bore evidence of torture inflicted in the Lubyanka, a 'laboratory of cruelty'.[31]

As an aside, it is interesting that Engels sometimes had a keener appreciation of the English legal system than Vyshinsky (or for that matter Pritt when he compared it unfavourably with the Soviet system). Writing in *The Role of Force in History* in 1888, and deploring that German law gave inadequate protection against police brutality, he concluded that England's two revolutions in the seventeenth century had prevented the creation of a police state with the result that English law 'culminated in two centuries of uninterrupted development of civil liberty.'[32]

Within two months of the Metro-Vickers trial ending, a conspiracy involving 85 officials was discovered in the People's Commissariat of Agriculture and State Farming. Their 'crime' was wrecking tractors in order to create a famine in the countryside – something which, as we shall see, Stalin had already accomplished. Thirty-five of them were shot, 22 received the standard 10-year sentence and 18 of them, eight years.[33]

It was following the Metro-Vickers trial that the office of Prosecutor-General of the USSR was created by decree with, in theory, a power of supervision over all courts,

---

31. *The Times*. 12 April 1933.
32. Engels. (London, Lawrence & Wishart Ltd., 1968), pp.102-3.
33. *Izvestia*. 12 March 1933.

police and other procurators nationwide. Unlike the procuracies of the republics the new all-union body was freed from control by the Commissariat of Justice and was made responsible only to the Party Central Committee. At this stage, Andrei Vyshinsky was appointed to be the first deputy but he subsequently took over as head of the Procuracy two years later, in June 1935, in time for the major show trials in which he became infamous for his reliance on 'confessions' produced by torture, his browbeating tactics and his violent language.

Features of all the early open trials were the falsity of the charges and the paucity of evidence. There was also inconsistency in testimony, when there was any, and inaccuracies in many of the prosecution allegations – weaknesses that had largely, but not entirely, been overcome by the time of the trials in 1936-38.

CHAPTER 4

War and Famine in the Countryside

Agricultural Policy

During the first five years of the New Economic Policy there had been a striking recovery in economic activity both in industry and on the country's farms. As part of the agricultural improvement the kulaks, who made up three to five per cent of the peasant households, had been producing around 20 per cent of the grain.[1] However, by 1927 the fixing at a low level of grain prices by the government resulted in it acquiring only 300 million poods[2] of grain at the end of the year in contrast to 428 million the previous year. As a result it was suggested by some Party members that kulaks and middle peasants were withholding deliveries until the spring when prices would be higher and that 150 million poods should be taken from them by force. To this Stalin responded in his report to the Fifteenth Party Congress in December 1927, in support of earlier advice by Lenin:

---

1. Robert Conquest. *The Harvest of Sorrow: Soviet Collectivization and the Terror-Famine.* (London, Arrow Books, 1988), p.75.
2. One pood was equal to approximately 15 kilograms.

Those comrades are wrong who think that it is possible and necessary to put an end to the kulaks by means of administrative measures, through the GPU: give an order, affix a seal, and that settles it. That is an easy way, but it is far from being effective. The kulak must be defeated by means of economic measures and in conformity with Soviet law. Soviet law, however, is not a mere phrase. This does not, of course, preclude the taking of certain necessary administrative measures against the kulaks. But administrative measures must not take the place of economic measures.[3]

The Congress decided against speedy mass collectivization and compulsory requisitioning of grain from well-to-do peasants but its resolution was not put into effect despite the protests of Bukharin, Rykov and Tomsky. The reason is clear. Stalin had spoken about raising tribute (capital) from the peasantry (rather like Britain had done with her colonies, he said)[4] to pay for industrialization and a few days after the end of the Congress, in a clear breach of its resolution, he sent out instructions to local Party leaders to secure a decisive breakthrough in grain procurement. This produced a campaign of violence with massive confiscations of land and personal possessions from, and brutality towards, many peasants across the country,

---

3.   Stalin. *Collected Works*. (London, Lawrence & Wishart, 1955), vol.x, p.319.
4.   Stalin. *Ibid.*

which in turn produced widespread peasant resistance.[5] As a consequence, a further drop in the sales of grain to the state resulted and, with strongly voiced opposition in the Party, Stalin temporarily backtracked, but to no avail once the plan had been set in motion. With grain prices kept artificially low peasants turned to other agricultural products, added to which hoarding and panic buying resulted from a war scare.

Contradicting his earlier statement to the Congress, Stalin now made a serious admission to the Party organization in Leningrad on 13 July 1928. 'Well,' he said, 'the grain had to be secured. Hence the renewed recourse to emergency measures, the arbitrary administrative measures, the infringements of revolutionary law, the house-to-house visitations, the unlawful searches and so on, which worsened the political situation in the country.'[6] In spite of this, he then made the situation even worse by threatening the kulaks with article 107 of the RSFSR criminal code.[7] This provided for imprisonment and confiscation of property for 'speculation' and had not previously been invoked since the 'crime' of speculation was not contrary to, and was indeed officially encouraged by, NEP policy. Fearing the worst when the threat would be made good, many kulaks sold their machinery and middle peasants hesitated to increase their productivity

---

5.   For its various forms cf. Sheila Fitzpatrick. *Stalin's Peasants: Resistance and Survival in the Russian Village after Collectivization.* (New York, Oxford University Press, 1994).
6.   Stalin. *Op. cit.* (London, Lawrence & Wishart, 1954), vol.xi, p.215.
7.   *Ibid.*, p.5.

through fear of being labelled 'kulaks'.

On 30 September 1928 Bukharin published in *Pravda* an article entitled 'Notes of an Economist'. In it he advocated restrictions on kulaks, development of co-operatives and a better price policy but rejected the proposed rapid industrialization at the expense of agriculture and the idea of a second revolution. Although he did not say so, it was a direct attack on Stalin's policy.

Collectivization

As part of the First Five-Year-Plan some forced, but moderate, collectivization involving the restriction of the kulaks as a class had been embarked upon. What constituted a 'kulak' was never clearly defined but he was loosely classified as a relatively well-to-do peasant who not only worked on his farm but also employed farm labourers and in some cases hired out machinery. In reality, kulaks, who, as we have seen, made up only three to five per cent of the peasant population, often had an income lower than that of rural officials and many poor and middle peasants were included in the classification, particularly if they had reservations about joining a collective farm or were church-goers.

It was in a situation of declining grain procurements, brought about by himself and the Party, that Stalin decided upon forcing all the peasantry into collective farms and 'eliminating the kulaks as a class', against the re-commendations of commissions set up to consider how to proceed, and again against opposition from Bukharin, Rykov and Tomsky who foresaw and feared what was about to happen.

As it was laid down in Stalin's 1938 *History of the CPSU(B) – Short Course*, at the end of 1929 the Soviet government turned sharply from the policy of restricting the kulaks to one of eliminating them as a class. The laws on the renting of land and the hiring of labour were repealed, and, it euphemistically claimed, the peasants were allowed to confiscate cattle, machines and other farm property from the kulaks for the benefit of the collective farms. The kulaks were expropriated and this, it said, was a profound revolution accomplished *from above*, on the initiative of the state, and directly supported *from below* by millions of peasants.[8] Despite the falsity of the last claim, in part these measures accounted for an expansion of state purchases of grain in 1930, but they were not repeatable. They also spelt the end of the NEP although this was never formally admitted.

Kulaks were not allowed to join the collective farms and by decrees, particularly article 107, their property could be confiscated and they and their families deported if they failed to supply the quota of agricultural produce fixed by the authorities. But even the qualification of these decrees was ignored by the enforcers of collectivization and, as a consequence, during the reign of terror of the expropriation campaign, out of 25 million peasant families, something

---

8. *History of the Communist Party of the Soviet Union (B) - (Short Course).* (Moscow, Foreign Languages Publishing House, 1939), pp.304-5.

like 10 million people in 'kulak' households were deported to the camps[9] where about a third of them perished. At one point 18 per cent of the Soviet labour force was made up of deportees. In the countryside legality was by-passed in a lawless reign of terror which engulfed the most productive peasants and caused widespread famine. Families were pitilessly left to starve in the streets and many children were taken from their parents and joined the wandering criminal bands that became a feature of Soviet life for many years. Indeed, with cannibalism acknowledged in the countryside, but not elsewhere, posters were actually put up in the Ukraine urging that it was wrong to eat dead children.[10]

In the process OGPU and Party officials resorted more and more to the use of violence to force the peasants to join collective farms. 'Can we permit,' asked Stalin, 'the expropriation of kulaks? A ridiculous question ... You do not lament the loss of the hair of one who has been beheaded ... We must break down the resistance of that class in open battle.'[11] As one historian has put it, 'the term *kulak* in the early 1930s produced much the same reaction among convinced communists as "jew" did in Nazi Germany; that is as vermin, subhuman enemies of the

---

9. Moshe Lewin. *Russian Peasants and Soviet Power*. London, George Allen & Unwin, 1968, pp.507-8. And S. Swianiewicz. *Forced Labour and Economic Development: An Inquiry into the Experience of Soviet Industrialization*. (London, Oxford University Press, 1965), p.124.
10. Beryl Williams. *Soviet Historians and the Rediscovery of the Soviet Past. Op. cit.*, p.230.
11. Isaac Deutscher. *Op. cit.*, p.320.

state to be shown no mercy. Stalin himself referred to them as "bloodsuckers, spiders and vampires".[12] After all, had not Lenin in the summer of 1918 said, 'The kulaks are the rabid foes of the soviet government ... These bloodsuckers have grown rich on the hunger of the people ... These spiders have grown fat at the expense of the peasants ... Ruthless war on the kulaks! Death to all of them.'[13] And, indeed, few of them at that time survived the period of War Communism.

In the result collectivization, which had a dynamic of its own, was carried through like a military operation. At this time the OGPU did indeed resemble an army, but unlike an army it was given wide legal powers to carry out summary executions and deport people to labour camps, openly described in one decree as concentration camps. This was when the Gulag (the Main Camp Administration) and massive slave labour came into their own. In fact, although for much of the time before 1937 terror and law were administered by separate agencies, during the first collectivization drive of winter and spring 1930 a district court in the Urals sentenced dozens of persons to death in hearings without witnesses and held *in camera* in the absence of the accused.[14]

Indeed, the problem became so serious that in March 1930 Stalin was forced to face up to the consequences and try to distance himself from the causes. Prior to obtaining

---

12. Beryl Williams. *Op. cit.*, p.229.
13. Figes. *Op. cit.*, p.618.
14. Peter H. Solomon Jr. *Soviet Criminal Justice and the Great Terror. Slavic Review.* vol. 46.1. Spring 1987, pp.391-2.

Politburo approval, he published a statement, inappropriately called 'Dizzy with Success', in which he said that collectivization was succeeding and now included half of all farms, but peasants should not be made to join by force. He pleaded that he had been misunderstood and officials were to blame.[15] An exodus of peasants who had newly joined the farms followed, with the numbers of households in them falling from some 14 million to just under six million in four months.

This gives some idea of the coercion to which the peasants had been subjected. However, they were not given back their land and livestock and soon many of them were forced to rejoin by starvation, outright pressure and very high quotas which if not met resulted in deportation to the camps. At the same time internal passports were made mandatory to prevent the voluntary movement of peasants. By 1931, 50 per cent of peasant households had finally been forced into the collective farms, and before long all of them. By then up to seven million people had died and 25 million peasant holdings had been replaced by 250,000 collective farms many of which were without the mechanized equipment with which they were supposed to become productive.

During the terror the reaction was such that the peasants had rebelled and 18 million horses, 30 million large cattle and some 100 million sheep and goats died or in some cases were slaughtered rather than be taken into the hated collective farms or because peasants did not

---

15. Stalin. *Collected Works.* vol.xii, pp.197-205.

want to be termed kulaks. Huge areas of land were left untilled and a deliberately created famine swept through the countryside.[16] According to Robert Conquest, in *The Harvest of Sorrow*,[17] the Ukraine and adjoining areas, with some 40 million inhabitants, were 'like one vast Belsen' (a description borne out by contemporary photographs). 'A quarter of the rural population,' he wrote, 'men, women and children, lay dead or dying - the numbers higher than the total deaths for all countries in the First World War.'

Tens of thousands of Party members and young communists (Komsomols) poured into the countryside to assist in forced collectivization and although they saw the effects of the famine they largely remained unmoved, or even enthusiastic. Yet its psychological effects upon them must have been lasting as is revealed in Victor Kravchenko's book, *I Chose Freedom*.[18] It is significant that Stalin refused to allow foreign newspapermen to travel from Moscow to the affected areas, although a few managed to do so and reported what they saw to general disbelief in the West, so terrible was the picture they painted. Butter was manufactured for export while babies swelled and died because there was no milk for them.[19] And to provide foreign capital for industry the export of grain had risen from 289,000 tons in 1927-8 and 178,000 tons in 1929-30, to 5,071,000 tons in 1931 and still

---

16. Deutscher. *Op. cit.*, p.325.
17. Conquest. *Op. cit.*, p.3.
18. (London, Robert Hale Ltd., 1947).
19. Swianiewicz. *Op. cit.*, p.89.

1,728,000 tons in 1932 and 1,686,000 tons in 1933.[20]

Abuse of Law and Genocide

In June 1930, even the hard-line state prosecutor, Nicolai Krylenko, had complained at the Sixteenth Party Congress about seizures of property, imprisonments and deportations being carried out in abuses of the legal code. Prosecutors, he said, who protested at being by-passed were accused of right-wing deviationism and removed from office. The judiciary, of which he was the head, functioned, he admitted, as an adjunct to the administrative apparatus.[21]

But his protest was ignored since this was being done in the name of the law which was itself deliberately being used to legitimize political terror. For example, a decree of February 1930 permitted local *administrative* authorities to 'take *all necessary measures* ... to fight kulaks, including confiscation of their property and deportation to the labour camps.'[22]

Furthermore, despite Stalin's attempt to shift the blame in 'Dizzy with Success', his other statements were used by the leading jurist, Andrei Vyshinsky, to defend the illegality under Soviet law of de-kulakization by arguing that the interests of the proletarian dictatorship were

---

20. Swianiewicz. *Op. cit.*, p.89.
21. Lewin. *Op. cit.*, pp.504-5.
22. *Ideas and Forces in Soviet Legal History*, pp.166-68.

superior to its own laws and outside the framework of any fixed legal system.[23]

Although forced collectivization was widespread throughout the Soviet Union, during its implementation in the Ukraine Stalin also carried out a purge of leading intellectuals and Party leaders in an effort to destroy Ukrainian nationalism. Involving as it did the destruction of a large segment of the population this amounted to genocide. Later, the United Nations Convention on the Prevention and Punishment of the Crime of Genocide, adopted on 9 December 1948 and ratified by the Soviet Union in 1954, confirmed that genocide, whether committed in time of peace or time of war, is a crime under international law. It defines genocide as 'acts committed with intent to destroy, in whole or in part, a national, ethnic, racial or religious group.' Such acts are stated to include 'killing members of the group' or 'deliberately inflicting on the group conditions of life calculated to bring about its physical destruction in whole or in part.' And not only genocide itself is punishable but also conspiracy, incitement and attempts to commit genocide.[24]

One response in the Soviet Union to forced collectivization was the Riutin Memorandum in August 1932. In this Riutin, a former Party secretary in Moscow, referred to Stalin's 'personal dictatorship' and claimed that he had changed his principles even more shamelessly than

---

23. A.Y. Vyshinsky. *Revolutionary Legality on the Present Stage.* (Moscow, State Publishing House, 1933), p.55.
24. United Nations General Assembly Resolution 260 (III).

bourgeois governments did and had offered a 'theoretically illiterate' idea on the development of agriculture. Stalin, he wrote, 'is killing Leninism, the proletarian Revolution under the flag of the proletarian Revolution and socialist construction under the flag of socialist construction.'[25] He called for the destruction of Stalin's dictatorship and, not surprisingly, was arrested in September 1932 when Stalin demanded that he be executed. It is believed however, although not proved, that the Politburo was divided with Kirov, Ordzhonikidze and others who, following Lenin, were opposed to the death penalty for Party leaders, and he was sent to the Gulag where he survived until the Great Terror and Stalin got his wish. Once again Zinoviev and Kamenev were expelled from the Party, this time for having received copies of one of Ruitin's works and not informing the authorities.[26]

---

25. Quoted in Robert W. Thurston. *Life and Terror in Stalin's Russia.* (New Haven, Yale University Press, 1996), p.16.
26. Tucker. *Stalin in Power. Op. cit.*, p.211.

CHAPTER 5

Law Legitimizing Terror

The Notorious Article 58

As we have seen, in order to achieve collectivization the law on land ownership had been changed overnight. Pashukanis argued that Soviet legislation should have maximum elasticity, not stability (as Stalin was later to require to Pashukanis's cost), since 'we have a system of proletarian politics, but we have no need for any sort of juridical system of proletarian law.' Asked by Stuchka, who was more moderate and had tried to promote a somewhat stable legal structure during the NEP, 'what of revolutionary legality?' he replied, 'for us revolutionary legality is a problem which is 99 per cent political.'[1]

This policy had been clearly expressed in the draconian article 58 of the criminal code of 1926[2] headed 'Counter-Revolutionary Crimes' which it should be noted replicated a draft prepared by Lenin for the 1922 RSFSR code. As we have seen, for Lenin law and the courts were a means of

---

1. *The Situation on the Legal Theory Front.* In Hugh W. Babb. *Soviet Legal Philosophy. Op. cit.*, pp.279-80.
2. The article is reproduced in full in Appendix G in Robert Conquest. *The Great Terror.* (London, Pelican Books, 1971), pp.741-46.

executing Party policy, including terror, and what he had had in mind in this instance, was made crystal clear in a letter he sent to the Commissar of Justice in the spring of 1922 urging that the definition of counter-revolutionary activity should be:

> A politically truthful (and not only a juridically narrow) proposition, giving the grounds for and justification of terror, its necessity, its limits.
>
> The courts should not eliminate terror – to promise that would be self-deception or deception – but should give it a legitimate basis, principled, clear, without hypocrisy or adornment. The formulation must be as broad as possible, for only a Revolutionary sense of the law and Revolutionary conscience will provide the conditions for a wider or narrower application in each case.[3]

The concept, which accordingly was broad enough to cover any act, or failure to act, of which the Party disapproved, was used by Lenin, and later by Stalin, to mask their destruction of legal process with an appearance of legality. The 'jurisprudence of terror', of which the article was part, meant that 'Legal forms were co-opted for extralegal purposes, judicial process was subordinated to political ends, and law itself was used to legitimize and rationalize terror. The jurisprudence of terror institutionalized and rendered routine political terror within the context of

---

3.   Lenin. *Collected Works. Op. cit.*, vol.xxxiii, pp.358-9.

formal legalism.'[4]

The article was mentioned frequently by those who managed to survive its application such as Nadezhda Mandelstam in her moving book *Hope against Hope,*[5] and was castigated by Alexander Solzhenitsyn who wrote 'In all truth there is no step, thought, action, or lack of action under the heavens which could not be punished by the heavy hand of article 58.'[6] In his anguish, and with withering scorn, Solzhenitsyn has written in detail of the many sections of the article and some of what he says is as follows:[7]

From 1934 on, when we were given back the term *Motherland*, subsections were inserted on *treason to the Motherland* – 1a,1b,1c,1d.

Broadly interpreted: when our soldiers were sentenced to only 10 years for allowing themselves to be taken prisoner (action injurious to Soviet military might), this was humanitarian to the point of being illegal. According to the Stalinist code, they should all have been shot on their return home.

One important additional broadening of the section on treason was its application 'via article 19 of the "Criminal Code" – via intent.' In other words, no treason had taken

---

4. Robert Sharlet. *Stalinism and Soviet Legal Culture.* In Robert C. Tucker, ed. *Stalinism: Essays in Historical Interpretation.* (New York, W.W. Norton & Co., 1977), p.164.
5. (London, Collins & Harvill Press, 1971).
6. Alexander Solzhenitsyn. *The Gulag Archipelago.* (London, Collins & Harvill, 1974), vol.i, p.60.
7. *Ibid.,* pp.60-67. Translated by Thomas P. Whitney. Harper & Row, Publishers, Inc.

place: but the interrogator envisioned an *intention* to betray
– and that was enough to justify a full term, the same as for
actual treason.

Section 6 was espionage.

This section was interpreted so broadly that if one were
to count up all those sentenced under it one might conclude
that during Stalin's time our people supported life not by
agriculture or industry, but only by espionage on behalf of
foreigners, and by living on subsidies from foreign intelligence
services.

Section 7 applied to subversion of industry, transport, trade and the circulation of money.

In the thirties, extensive use was made of this section to
catch masses of people – under the catchword *wrecking* ... For
centuries the people had built and created, always honorably,
always honestly, even for serf-owners and nobles. Yet no one
had ever heard of *wrecking*. But now, when for the first time
all the wealth had come to belong to the people, hundreds of
thousands of the best sons of the people inexplicably rushed
off to *wreck*.

Section 8 covered terror (not that terror from above for which the Soviet Criminal Code was supposed to 'provide a foundation and basis in legality',[8] but terrorism from below).

Terror was construed in a very broad sense to include an
assault on a personal enemy if he was an activist in the Party.
And the concept was extended by the same article 19, i.e.,

---

8. Lenin. *Collected Works. Op. cit.* Fifth edition, vol.45, p.190.

intent in the sense of *preparation*, to include not only a direct threat against an activist uttered near a beer hall ('Just you wait!') but also the quick-tempered retort of a peasant woman at the market ('Oh, drop dead!'). Both qualified as TN –Terrorist Intent – and provided a basis for applying the article in all its severity. This sounds like an exaggeration, a farce, but it was not I who invented that farce. I was in prison with these individuals.

Section 10 dealt with 'Propaganda or agitation, containing an appeal for the overthrow, subverting or weakening of the soviet power ... and, equally, the dissemination or preparation or possession of literary materials of similar content.' No upper limit was set for the maximum penalty.

This was held to include a face-to-face conversation between friends or even between husband and wife, or a private letter. The term 'preparation of literary materials' covered every letter, note or private diary, even when only the original document existed. Thus happily expanded, what *thought* was there, whether merely in the mind, spoken aloud, or jotted down, which was not covered by section 10 under which no upper limit was set for the maximum penalty?

Section 12 dealt with the failure to make a denunciation of any action of the type listed. Again, there was no maximum limit for the penalty.

This section was in itself such a fantastic extension of everything else that no further extension was needed. *He knew and he did not tell* became the equivalent of 'He did it himself!'

Solzhenitsyn might have added that the various extended meanings given to most of the sections of the article were made by unannounced decisions, which in themselves deepened the general atmosphere of fear. Indeed, in his book *The First Circle* he was to write that 'by 1949 the criminal code of 1926, although still valid, had been effectively replaced by a batch of important directives, and most of them secret, and known only by code numbers (eg, 083, or 005, 2748).'[9]

In any event, in *The Gulag Archipelago* he rightly concluded that the 'damascene steel of article 58, first tried out in 1927, right after it was forged, was whetted by all the waves of the following decade, and with whistle and slash was used to the full to deal telling blows in *the law's attack upon the people in 1937*'[10] (author's italics).

Even so, the article and its extensions were not considered sufficient by Stalin. After the assassination of Kirov on 1 December 1934 the RSFSR Code of Criminal Procedure of 1923 was amended to encourage the authorities to expedite cases involving alleged terrorism by individuals or groups. And in the same year the notorious special board of the NKVD (the People's Commissariat of Internal Affairs) absorbed the OGPU and was exempted from all the procedural requirements of both the codes of criminal law and those of procedure. The board dealt with cases where there was insufficient evidence to go before a court and before it the defendants

---

9.   (London, Fontana Books, 1970), pp.442-3.
10.   Solzhenitsyn. *The Gulag Archipelago. Op. cit.*, p.68.

had no right of defence, the cases were heard *in camera*, and usually without the accused being present. Gradually its sentencing powers were increased from a maximum of five years to 25 years. Article 58 was not repealed until December 1958.

The Smolensk Archives[11]

In July 1941 the German army occupied Smolensk, a city standing on both banks of the Dnieper River some 260 miles west of Moscow. There they captured Party records covering the period 1917-1939, subsequent files having been burnt or removed to the capital. It is a shortcoming that they are confined to one region and are a random selection made by German intelligence. But they covered an area of nearly 20,000 square miles with a population of six and a half million people and are revealing about the processes of local government and Party purges in the Soviet Union over those 22 years. More than 500 files were rescued containing some 200,000 pages of documents which were shipped to Germany where they fell into the hands of the United States army in 1945 and were housed in Washington DC before being microfilmed and sold to libraries around the world.

The archives confirm that once Stalin's forced collectivization was started the Procuracy and the courts

---

11. For a full account of the Smolensk Archives see Merle Fainsod. *Smolensk under Soviet Rule.* (London, Macmillan & Co. Ltd., 1958).

discarded any pretence of upholding legality and openly joined the forces of oppression. Nevertheless, as elsewhere, repressive measures got out of hand. For example, on 26 October 1929 the deputy procurator of the western region of Smolensk sent an order to other procurators which read in part: 'Taking into account that we recently applied measures of coercion, as a result of which we have an overload of the places of detention, it is necessary immediately to switch and apply pressure along the lines of economic coercion (fines, confiscation, and exile).' Further, overzealous militiamen were instructed to 'approach the question of detention more carefully, especially in cases of counter-revolutionary agitation and propaganda where, at times, they jail a poor peasant because he somewhere shouted a phrase against soviet authority.' Even then the case had to be sent to the OGPU.[12] In the event, such orders had little effect as the archives and a secret memorandum of the People's Commissar of Justice testified.[13]

As for Stalin's repeated claims that only kulaks were to be liquidated as a class whilst middle and poor peasants were to be helped, the archives show that during February 1930 alone the courts in just one area of the region handled 509 cases concerned with collectivization which involved 911 persons, of whom 858 were convicted. Of those, 298 were classified as kulaks, 194 as well-to-do peasants, 230 as middle peasants, 48 as poor peasants and

12. *Ibid.*, p.180.
13. *Ibid.*

46 as officials. Into what category the remaining 40 were to be found is not recorded.

The largest group of cases involved alleged the slaughter of cattle, followed by 'counter-revolutionary' agitation against collectivization, as well as hooliganism at meetings. Judges who were found to be sympathetic to measures taken by kulaks to protect themselves, their families and their property were purged. On the other hand, sometimes courts were found to have dealt too harshly with middle and poor peasants. But in all cases it was necessary for both the procurators and the courts, on the occasions when they were involved, to follow Stalin's policy and demands.

How far matters were out of hand, even as late as 1933, is revealed by a secret letter sent by Stalin and Molotov on 8 May of that year addressed to all Party workers and to all organs of the OGPU, the courts and the Procuracy which read:

The Central Committee and the Council of Commissars are informed that disorderly mass arrests in the countryside are still a part of the practice of our officials. Such arrests are made by chairmen of collective farms and members of collective farm administrations, by chairmen of village Soviets and secretaries of Party cells, by district officials; arrests are made by all who desire to, and who, strictly speaking, have no right to make arrests. It is not surprising that in such a saturnalia of arrests, organs which do have the right to arrest, including the organs of the OGPU and especially the militia lose all feeling of moderation and often perpetrate arrests without any basis, acting according to the rule: 'First arrest, and then investigate.'[14]

The Courts and Crime in Smolensk[15]

So far as legality is concerned the Smolensk archives reveal that despite their zeal, members of the regional Party and the Procuracy frequently found themselves helpless, and often victims, in the face of NKVD terror. Many Party leaders, members of the Procuracy and regional judges were declared to be Trotskyists and enemies of the people who had violated revolutionary legality and carried out wrecking activities in the courts. They were arrested by the NKVD and summarily dealt with. Not surprisingly, one of the men who rose rapidly in the Party as a result of his denunciations of others was himself denounced because the husband of his sister was an enemy of the people. The general picture which emerges is of the subservience of the Procuracy and the courts as tools of the Party rather than guardians of legality they were supposed to uphold.

As far as crime is concerned, as already noted the NKVD absorbed, and was established by the Politburo as successor to, the OGPU in 1934, with the militia, for the

---

14. *Ibid.*, p.185.
15. *Ibid.*, p.180.

first time, under its control. The militia continued to deal with ordinary crimes whilst the NKVD concentrated on alleged crimes against the state. An attempt was made to restrict the activities of the NKVD by giving the newly established national Procuracy power to supervise the legality of its methods but this proved futile as legal forms lost their significance.

The files reveal that banditry was a major problem and one case, heard on 16 January 1934, dealt with armed bandits who, over a period of three weeks, had been involved in 13 street robberies in which one person was shot. Two of the bandits had previous criminal records and the rest were young factory workers of whom four were members of the Komsomol (Young Communist League) and one the son of a Party member. On the same day another bandit group was captured by the militia after having robbed peasant homes, stolen collective farm horses and murdered a peasant woman who refused to hand over gold they believed she possessed. They were armed with a revolver, three hunting rifles and knives and one of the group was a Komsomol secretary. Another armed band was provided with hiding places by a chairman of a village Soviet and two village Soviet members who shared in the spoils of the robberies. According to the records the local peasants knew what was going on but were too terrorized to reveal it or even report crimes of which they were themselves the victims.

Similarly, the militia was engaged in a constant battle against arson, usually involving state or collective farm property. Stealing from the farms and their warehouses was also rampant as was embezzlement in state enterprises. During the period the militia also investigated cases of attacks on Soviet officials and, in some cases, violence by officials on peasants and their wives. Such were the types of crimes generated under Stalin's dictatorship by people who felt themselves alienated by the regime.

As shown earlier, even the Party was not immune from purges and this was confirmed by the weeding out of 'demoralized' members in 1929-30 and 1933 for crimes, violations of discipline and refusal to join collective farms alleged against them by informers who stood to gain promotion by their disappearance. After the assassination of Kirov in 1934, and again in 1936 at the commencement of the Great Terror the archives give graphic details of the widespread hunt for enemies in the Party following orders from on high. As a part of Soviet culture people were encouraged to voice complaints and in this case a wave of denunciations swept through Party ranks giving rise to growing panic as leaders and rank-and-file members alike were 'unmasked' as traitors and spies.

CHAPTER 6

Trial by Terror

Assassination of Kirov

Sergei Kirov was the popular head of the Party in Leningrad. Although he fully supported Party policy he exhibited traits of independence and was somewhat more moderate than Stalin who might have seen him as a serious rival for power particularly after he secured 300 more votes than Stalin at the Seventeenth Party Congress in January 1934.[1] It is said that when Stalin argued in the Politburo for imposing the death penalty on the supporters of the Riutin Memorandum, Kirov was among those who blocked it.[2] Yet at that same Party Congress Kirov said, 'It seems to me, comrades, that as a result of this detailed consideration of the report of the Central Committee which has taken place in this Congress, it would be useless to think what kind of resolution to adopt on the report of comrade Stalin. It will be more correct, and more useful for the work at hand, to accept as Party law all the

---

1. Conquest. *Stalin and the Kirov Murder*. (London, Hutchinson, 1989), p.29.
2. Roy Medvedev. *Op. cit.*, pp.329-330.

proposals and considerations of comrade Stalin's speech.'[3] The delegates voted to adopt this suggestion in place of the usual resolution.

As historian Adam B. Ulam has commented, 'This was unprecedented. It conferred upon Stalin virtually all the powers and attributes possessed by the Congress, the sovereign body of the Communist Party. If before it was barely conceivable that he might be dismissed by the Central Committee it now became unthinkable: even in theory he was no longer its servant but its master.'[4] Yet this was a period in which Stalin, through Litvinov, was courting the Western democracies rather than Nazi Germany and took the Soviet Union into the League of Nations, whilst the Politburo was apparently relaxing repression at home. The number of arrests decreased, Bukharin was partially restored to favour and living standards were slowly improving.

Then, suddenly, on 1 December 1934, Kirov was murdered at the Smolny headquarters of the Communist Party, a vast classical palace and former aristocratic girls' school in Leningrad where Kirov had his offices. The assassin was Leonid Nikolayev, a disgruntled Party member. Astonishingly, no guards were around at the time and Kirov's personal bodyguard, Borisov, had apparently been detained some way away.

It is widely believed that Stalin was the brains behind

---

3. *Report of the Seventeenth Congress of the All-Union Communist Party.* (Moscow, State Publishing House, 1934), p.251.
4. Adam B. Ulam. *Stalin: The Man and his Era.* (London, I.B. Tauris & Co., Ltd., 1989), p.372.

the assassination and there is circumstantial evidence to support that belief although it cannot be proved beyond all doubt. Nevertheless by 1988 Soviet historians and others were beginning to accept the dictator's guilt.[5] Nicolayev had earlier been arrested twice and on one occasion found in possession of a revolver and a map of Kirov's route to his office. Incredibly, on both occasions he was released, once on orders from Moscow where Yagoda, head of the NKVD, had sent instructions to Ivan Zaporozhets, the second-in-command of the Leningrad NKVD, to remove all obstacles to the assassination. This was admitted by Yagoda in his subsequent trial when he sought to blame Abel Yenukidze, who was secretary of the Central Executive Committee but subordinate to Yagoda. In any event, it is inconceivable that such instructions should have been given by either Yagoda or Yenukidze without Stalin's knowledge or orders. It is said that in fact Zaporozhets or a deputy of his provided Nikolayev with the gun and had a friend persuade him to choose Kirov as his target.[6]

On the day of Kirov's death security at the Smolny was uncharacteristically lax and after his death key witnesses, including the loyal Borisov who had become suspicious, were killed in unusual circumstances. According to Khrushchev in his secret speech to the Twenty-Second Party Congress in 1956, when Borisov was being taken for

---

5. Conquest. *Stalin and the Kirov Murder. Op. cit.*, pp.136-7.
6. Alexander Orlov. *The Secret History of Stalin's Crimes.* (New York, Random House, 1953), pp.29-30.

questioning by Stalin, Molotov and Voroshilov, 'he was killed in a car "accident" in which no other occupants of the car were harmed. After the murder of Kirov, top functionaries of the Leningrad NKVD were given very light sentences, but in 1937 they were shot. We can assume that they were shot in order to cover the traces of the organizers of Kirov's killing.'[7] After 'confessing' to participating in an alleged Zinovievite opposition group Nikolayev was tried in secret and, with his wife, executed. The suggestion that any Zinovievist group would want to kill such a popular leader as Kirov makes no sense if they wished to replace Stalin.

In 1956 Khrushchev set up a Commission of Inquiry into the exact circumstances of the murder. Its members had access to all the archives and interviewed hundreds of witnesses but its report has never been published. However, in an extract from his memoirs published in 1989 Khrushchev said, 'I believe that the murder was organized by Yagoda, who could have taken this action only on secret instructions from Stalin, received face to face.'[8] In 1991 the last surviving member of that Commission, Olga Shatunovskaya, was interviewed on British television.[9] She says that at the Seventeenth Party Congress in 1934 there were moves to replace Stalin as General Secretary of the Party with Kirov, although the latter refused to stand. She claims that in the archives the

---

7. Khrushchev. *Op. cit.,* p.575.
8. See Alan Bullock. *Hitler and Stalin: Parallel Lives.* (London, Harper Collins, 1991), p.520.
9. *In the Time of Stalin.* (Thames Television, 1991), vol.2, part 12.

Commission unsealed the ballot papers of that Congress and found that the result announced in Stalin's favour was false, but the Commission's report was suppressed and shredded. She also says that 'It's been proved incontrovertibly that Kirov's murder was organized by Stalin' but her full statement on television, although extremely persuasive, does not prove that incontrovertibly.

In any event, what is important is that whether or not Stalin had any part in the murder he took advantage of it to unleash the terror of succeeding years. Eugenia Ginzburg, who, after harrowing experiences in the camps still remained loyal to the Party when writing her book *Into the Whirlwind,* started it with the sentence, 'The year 1937 really began on 1 December 1934.'

On 5 December 1934, four days after Kirov's murder, *Pravda* published Stalin's instructions, which had been issued even earlier, that in cases involving terrorism investigations were to be completed in 10 days; indictments were to be shown to those accused only the day before the court hearing at which they were not to be present; sentences were not to be subject to appeal or pleas for clemency; and death sentences were to be carried out immediately. While the country was still in mourning for the dead leader, this edict was put into instant effect with executions of 104 alleged White Guard terrorists, said to have infiltrated from abroad, and others who had been taken prisoner before the assassination had taken place. Then, according to Alexander Orlov, the explanation that White Guards had carried out the assassination was quickly abandoned, although not before the executions, and the 'Zinoviev-Trotsky opposition' blamed instead.[10]

Roy Medvedev says of Orlov's book, *The Secret History of Stalin's Crimes*, that it was not always reliable as he often used rumours and chance conversations as sources, although he accepts that 'on the whole the book is an important document.'[11] In fact, Orlov not only served in the Red Army during the civil war but became an assistant prosecutor at the Supreme Court and took part in preparing the first Soviet criminal code. Furthermore, he was a senior member of the OGPU and NKVD and broke with Stalin whilst in Spain where he had been sent by the Politburo as an adviser to the republican government during the Spanish civil war. When Yagoda was arrested a large number of Orlov's colleagues in the secret police were liquidated.

In the spring of 1935 after Kirov's murder over 60,000 of Leningrad residents were transported to camps in Siberia and, as we have seen, top functionaries of the Leningrad NKVD were at first dealt with suspiciously leniently, only later to be shot in the Great Terror to prevent them speaking of what they knew of the assassination.

Following Kirov's death terrorist centres were alleged to exist in Leningrad and Moscow. Khrushchev, who was secretary of the Moscow Party Committee at the time, recalled being told by Redens, the chief of the Moscow NKVD and Stalin's brother-in-law, that he had received

---

10. *Cf.* Orlov. *Op. cit.*
11. Medvedev. *Let History Judge. Op. cit.*, p.360.

instructions to 'purge' Moscow.[12] Within three weeks of Kirov's death, on 22 December, it was decided to bring to trial Zinoviev and Kamenev (both of whom had worked closely with Lenin) with 17 others as leaders of a conspiracy to assassinate him. Their trial commenced in Moscow on 15-16 January 1935 with the cruel and subservient army military jurist, V.V. Ulrich, as the presiding judge and Vyshinsky the prosecutor.

The trial was held *in camera* and no account of the proceedings was issued but Zinoviev is said to have confessed that although many of those in the dock were not known to him he was ultimately responsible for the conspirators. And Kamenev declared that he did not know of the existence of the 'Moscow Centre', of which it was alleged he was an active member, but in so far as it existed he took responsibility for it.[13] In spite of the absence of any evidence against them apart from these ambiguous 'confessions', Zinoviev was sentenced to 10 years' imprisonment and Kamenev to five years.

In the spring of 1935 two decrees were issued which made it easier for the NKVD to exercise mental torture on accused persons. The first, dated 30 March and added to article 58, provided the death penalty for flight abroad and if the offender was a member of the military his relatives who were aware of the impending flight became liable to up to 10 years' imprisonment and those who knew nothing

---

12. *Khrushchev Remembers. Op. cit.*, p.78.
13. R. Conquest. *The Great Terror: A Reassessment.* (London, Hutchinson, 1990), pp.49

about it, but were living with him or dependent on him, were liable to five years exile. They were examples of the revived system of civilian hostage-taking. The second decree, dated 7 April, extended all penalties, including death, down to 12-year-old children[14] which facilitated pressure on accused persons awaiting trial.

The Moscow Show Trials

All the earlier trials were preparations for the bizarre show trials in Moscow in the years 1936-39, overseen by Stalin personally. As show trials they were portraying dramas in which all the participants operated as actors on a grand scale in a mockery of legality. By this time the NKVD had perfected its methods of physical torture as well as using the mental torture of threats against the lives of the loved ones of the victims. Nevertheless, it must be remembered that the vast majority of those who were tried at all, and most victims were shot summarily, had their cases dealt with *in camera* presumably because they did not confess. In each show case months of preparation went into settling the various scenarios for the courtroom and refining the contents of all the 'confessions' extracted from the accused – often physically and mentally strong men and devoted Bolsheviks.

Those who confessed under torture during their preliminary examinations but attempted to recant their

---

14. *Izvestia*. 8 April 1935.

'confessions' when brought into court were handed back to the NKVD during court adjournments and reappeared to withdraw their recantations. All played out their allotted parts except Bukharin who, against all the odds in his verbal battles with an angry Vyshinsky, managed to put across usually coded, but sometimes open, messages to those able and willing to read them. Nevertheless, dramatic as these trials were they were a cover for the millions sent to their deaths by the NKVD after trials behind closed doors or, in most cases, without any trial at all. Those who were publicly accused were made the scapegoats for the chronic shortages of food and other consumer goods, industrial failures, devastation in the countryside and lack of freedom, and for the blame from which Stalin sought to be absolved.

Zinoviev and Kamenev

For the first show trial the Old Bolsheviks Zinoviev and Kamenev were brought back to court again from the prison at Verkhne-Uralsk, and were tried with 14 alleged co-conspirators. They could have been left to die in prison, or even have had their deaths there accelerated, but Stalin wanted it to be seen that no one, not even Lenin's close associates, was to be safe from the unfolding Terror. Hence this time they were to be tried in public. The preparations were ready by June 1936 except that neither of the chief accused had yet confessed. However, Zinoviev was ill from heart and liver trouble and began to soften up under severe physical pressure, whilst Kamenev began to weaken when his son was threatened and an order for his arrest was given in Kamenev's presence in prison. Both of the principal accused then agreed to go into the dock and stand trial if Stalin would confirm in the presence of the Politburo his promises not to have them or their followers executed, and to allow their families to remain at liberty. Stalin confirmed his promises in the presence of a nominal Politburo consisting of himself, his old Tsaritzyn crony Klementi Voroshilov and NKVD official Nicholai Yezhov – which, of course, meant nothing.

Possibly to reassure wavering members of the Politburo who were concerned about the trials, and certainly to give confidence to, and secure 'confessions' from, those about to face trial, a decree was published on 11 August providing for hearings in public, for defence lawyers to be available and for an opportunity to appeal during the three days following sentence. Stalin was also at this time endeavouring to impress the West, where Communist Parties were attempting to form anti-fascist fronts (and supporting a Popular Front government in France) with his democratic credentials.

Four days later, on 15 August 1936, the trial began before the Military Collegium of the Supreme Court, in the small October Hall of the trade union headquarters in Moscow, with 30 foreign diplomats and journalists and 150 Russians approved by the NKVD present.[15] Stalin's

---

15. Max Shacktman. *Behind the Moscow Trial.* (New York, Pioneer Publishers, 1936), pp.1-142.

henchman Ulrich again presided with Vyshinsky prosecuting. The accused indicated that they did not want counsel, no doubt because in such trials defence counsel were likely to stress the guilt of their clients.

Zinoviev, Kamenev and those accused with them were charged with practising terrorism in league with Trotskyites contrary to article 58 of the criminal code; of assassinating Kirov; and of conspiring with Hitler's Germany to murder Stalin and other Soviet leaders and overthrow the regime. The last part of the charge, which was repeated in subsequent trials, was necessary to link the accused with Stalin's insistence that the class struggle had intensified as a result of capitalist encirclement of the Soviet Union. All except two of the defendants pleaded guilty. One of the accused, Holtzman, admitted that he was a member of a Trotskyist organization but denied that he condoned terrorism. He also said that he had met Trotsky's son in the Hotel Bristol in Copenhagen in 1932. Not until the hearing was over was it found that the hotel had been demolished in 1917.

In any event, it was at this time that Stalin was proclaiming that a classless society had been established in the Soviet Union and that it was a supreme joy to be living in the midst of a socialist society. Why then the accused, all of whom had devoted their lives to achieving socialism, should abandon their past ideals and actions and attempt to restore capitalism with the aid of the Nazis remained unanswered.

During the trial Vyshinsky issued a statement in which he said that some of the accused had referred to Bukharin,

Tomsky, Radek, Rykov and other Party leaders and Bolsheviks as being involved in the counter-revolutionary activities for which the accused were being tried. An investigation would be put in hand, he said, and in accordance with its results 'the office of the state attorney will institute proceedings.' Thus, without awaiting the outcome of the investigation, he gave notice of the forthcoming trial and execution of these Old Bolsheviks. Indeed for the veteran leader of the trade unions, Tomsky, death came sooner rather than later for on reading Vyshinsky's statement he committed suicide.

Another of the accused, Ivan Smirnov, was known as the 'Lenin of Siberia' for his part in leading the Bolshevik Revolution in that region. He denied taking part in terrorist activities but confessions of others implicated him – as was usual with 'confessions' in Soviet courts – and his family had been arrested. But that was not enough for Vyshinsky who, in his final speech for the prosecution, reminded the court that Smirnov had said that he had done nothing as he was in prison from 1 January 1933 for allegedly approving proposals to remove Stalin. 'A naïve assertion!' said Vyshinsky. 'We know that while in prison Smirnov organized contacts with his Trotskyites, for a code was discovered by means of which, while in prison, he communicated with his companions outside. This proves that communication existed and Smirnov cannot deny this.' However, no such code was ever produced even though the man's life was at stake and, if he had wished, Trotsky could have easily found a messenger not restrained and under surveillance in prison. Vyshinsky's peroration ended with the words, 'I demand that these dogs gone mad should be shot – every one of them!'[16]

Not surprisingly all the accused were found guilty and sentenced to death. Despite the terms of the August decree all were shot within 24 hours and Stalin's promises to Zinoviev and Kamenev about their followers and families were shown to be equally worthless. Kamenev's sons, one an air force pilot and the other a young boy, were sent to labour camps in the Gulag. Smirnov's daughter was imprisoned and his wife sent to a women's camp at Kotlas where she was shot in 1938 during a mass execution of 1,300 'undesirables'.

The window-dressing effect of the trial can be judged from the assessment of the then well-known British lawyer, D.N. Pritt, KC, who was present at the trial and wrote a pamphlet favourable to the court that was translated into seven or eight languages. Even as late as 1965, nine years after Khrushchev's revelations, he wrote in his autobiography that:

The trial was in general fairly conducted, and the accused were guilty. Vyshinsky, the prosecutor, certainly said hard things about the accused, if not as hard as those an English prosecutor would have said in a similar case; but he never bullied, and he never even raised his voice ... The impression of every journalist to whom I was able to speak was that the trial was fair, and the accused were guilty; and

---

16. *Ibid.*

certainly every foreign observer, of whom there were quite a few, mainly from the diplomatic corps, thought the same.[17]

Happily, not all observers saw the trial through the same prism however, and although Pritt was a Labour MP, after the trial the Labour Party published a pamphlet by an Austrian Social Democrat who described the proceedings as 'witchcraft' and asserted that Pritt had been hired by the Soviet Union to whitewash the trial. Pritt denied the allegation, but decided not to sue the author or the Labour Party for libel, in the main, he said, because 'the better elements of the working class – of whom there were of course many in the Labour Party – detest recourse to the courts.'[18]

Once the trial was over, a decree was issued on 14 September 1936 which for cases under article 58 (sections vii, viii and ix) of the criminal code forbade appeals and petitions for clemency as well as eliminating publicity in court trials. The last-named was not put into effect however until after the Bukharin trial in 1938. The decree was followed by another in October 1936 which increased the maximum term of imprisonment from 10 to 25 years.[19]

17. D.N. Pritt. *Autobiography: From Right to Left*. (London, Lawrence & Wishart Ltd., 1965), pp.110-114.

18. *Ibid.*

19. SZ. (1937) 66/297. (Collections of Laws and Regulations of the USSR).

The Trial of Pyatakov, Radek and Others

The second show trial was that of the so-called 'Anti-Soviet Trotskyite Centre' and was held from 23 January to 30 January 1937, again in the October Hall.[20] Among the 17 accused were Yuri Leonidovich Pyatakov, who presided over the 1922 trial of the Socialist Revolutionary Party but was now Deputy Commissar for Heavy Industry; Karl Radek, a puckish figure and highly regarded Soviet propagandist with a biting pen who had been Comintern head in Germany from 1918 to 1922, Grigory Yakovlevich Sokolnikov, a member of Lenin's first Politburo; and Leonid Serebryakov, former secretary of the Central Committee. All faced charges of treason, espionage, and the preparation of terrorist acts, again contrary to article 58 of the criminal code. It was further alleged that they had formed a Trotskyite 'parallel centre' aimed at seizing power with the aid of foreign states, particularly Germany and Japan, in order to restore capitalism and cede Soviet territory to those states. As previously indicated, since Stalin blamed the intensification of the class struggle inside the Soviet Union, where he claimed antagonistic classes no longer existed, on outside 'capitalist encirclement' it was clearly necessary for him to implicate the accused in foreign espionage. All the accused pleaded guilty, having already conceded their guilt in preliminary

---

20. Unless otherwise indicated the quotations that follow are taken from the verbatim transcript of the trials published by the People's Commissariat of Justice of the USSR in 1937 as *The Report of Court Proceedings in the Case of the Anti-Soviet Trotskyite Centre.*

examinations by the NKVD. It is a measure of the relentless pressure on them that the preparations for the trial had taken some 18 months.

The first to be questioned by Vyshinsky was Pyatakov, although the prosecutor would frequently draw in other defendants to make his point. In general, Pyatakov confessed to forming terrorist and sabotage groups but at no time did he admit to complicity in any of the specific acts of violence that were alleged against him. Certain acts of so-called sabotage he put down to negligence and bad planning. And as for his relations with Trotsky, Pyatakov said that in December 1935 when he was in Berlin, where he was engaged in Soviet government business, he met a courier of Trotsky's and had arranged to fly to an aerodrome in Oslo from where he was taken to a meeting with Trotsky in a country suburb. He added that in a two hour conversation Trotsky told him that war was imminent, the collapse of the Soviet Union inevitable and that a *coup d'état* was necessary. The following exchange then took place:

Vyshinsky: The conversation you had with Trotsky in December 1935 and the line he gave, did you accept it as a directive or simply as something said in a conversation, but not binding for you?
Pyatakov: Of course as a directive.
Vyshinsky: Hence, we can take it that you subscribed to it?
Pyatakov: We can take it that I carried it out.
Vyshinsky: And carried it out.
Pyatakov: Not 'and carried it out,' but 'carried it out.'
Vyshinsky: There is no difference in that whatever.

110

Pyatakov:　　There is to me.

It is a fine distinction but the essential point is that the direct link with Trotsky, on which all the cases really rested, was a fiction. In December 1935 Trotsky was certainly in Norway and Pyatakov in Berlin but they did not meet.

It was during the trial, on 25 January, that the Norwegian newspaper *Aftenposten* drew attention to the fact that no civil aircraft had landed at Oslo's airport during December 1935. And four days later the Norwegian social democratic newspaper *Arbeiderbladet* disclosed that no aircraft at all had landed there between September 1935 and May 1936.[21] Vyshinsky was clearly embarrassed and towards the end of the trial he made the rather weak point that the Soviet embassy in Oslo had received information that it was possible for the airport to receive planes in winter months. This was hardly confirmation that the newspapers were wrong and that one had in fact landed. This 'evidence' of Pyatakov's was of course a fabrication invented for him during his interrogation, similar to that about the Bristol Hotel in Copenhagen in the Zinoviev trial – and as reliable.

This did not prevent Dudley Collard, an English lawyer present during the trial, from writing in his book *Soviet Justice and the Trial of Radek and Others*, 'I have read some statement to the effect that no aeroplanes flew from Germany to Norway in December 1935. It seems hard to

---

21. R. Conquest. *The Great Terror: A Reassessment. Op. cit.*, pp.151-2.

believe that this is so, and one does not know, of course, whether "special" aeroplanes are referred to, or only civil air liners. In any case it is clear that everyone was interested in concealing this trip, and that highly placed persons were concerned in organizing it. It may be, therefore, that no record exists of the flight.'[22] Like D.N. Pritt earlier this experienced barrister, acting outside his own legal milieu, concluded that all the accused had received a fair trial and were guilty. To let the sceptical British public know this he wrote his account of the trial which was published by Victor Gollancz as part of his well-known Left Book Club series. How and why he came to be admitted into the court he did not reveal.

Radek was a more compliant witness and implicated his friend Bukharin, which is what Stalin required for the most important show trial which was to follow. In fact, in the absence of documents and real proofs the only 'evidence' produced at the trials were the 'confessions' of the defendants and their accusations against each other, first obtained when they were in the custody of the NKVD. At one point Radek indicated that after his arrest he had denied all the allegations against him for three months. 'Does not that,' asked Vyshinsky, 'cast doubt on what you said about your vacillations and misgivings?' To which Radek made the significant reply, 'Yes, if you ignore the fact that you learned about the programme and about Trotsky's instructions only from me, of course, it does cast doubt on what I have said.'

---

22. (London, Victor Gollancz Ltd., 1937), pp.52-3.

After the other accused had all given evidence incriminating themselves and each other Vyshinsky, in his final address to the court, said that it could be asked, in a case involving conspiracy and a programme, where are the documents, their decisions, rules and minutes? His reply was bold indeed. 'I am bold enough to assert,' he said, 'in keeping with the fundamental requirements of the science of criminal procedure, that in cases of conspiracy such demands cannot be put.' Raising his voice he then shouted:

> I do not stand here alone! The victims may be in their graves, but I feel that they are standing here beside me, pointing at the dock, at you, accused, with their mutilated arms, which have mouldered in the graves to which you sent them!
>
> I am not the only accuser! I am joined in my accusation by the whole of our people! I accuse these heinous criminals who deserve only one punishment – death by shooting!

Unlike those in the Zinoviev trial, the accused accepted defence counsel and they were permitted to speak. One example will suffice. S.K. Kaznacheyev, of the Moscow Collegium of Defence, in defending V.V. Arnold said, 'Comrade Judges, monstrous was the picture of treason and treachery which was unfolded before you in the course of these few days. The guilt of the accused in the dock is immeasurable in its gravity ... inasmuch as the path of these organizations leads over the dead bodies of workers, over the dead bodies of the finest sons of our soviet country – the mere fact of being a member of these organizations is a most heinous crime.' After mentioning that Arnold had served a sentence in America 'for some kind of talk about the soviet government' – an intriguing thought – he continued, 'At first glance it may appear strange that I, Arnold's defending counsel, should admit these facts' (i.e., taking part in the conspiracy). 'But, Comrade Judges, to pass something over in silence is the worst method of defence.'

The accused were allowed to debase themselves in final statements to the court, and when Radek began a sentence with the words 'Comrade Judges' he was admonished by Ulrich saying 'Accused Radek, not Comrade Judges', but 'Citizen Judges'. Following the predetermined verdicts all were sentenced to death except Sokolnikov, Radek and Arnold who were given 10 years each and Stroilov who got eight. Dudley Collard commented, 'In the result the court was more merciful than I would have been!'[23] Radek was probably saved from shooting because of his assistance to the prosecution and his implication of Bukharin but he was sent to the Gulag where he was killed by another prisoner in 1939 and Sokolnikov died in camp in the same year. In accordance with the normal practice, wives of several of the accused were also sent to the camps.

As a postscript to the trials, on 18 February Sergei Ordzhonikidze died, officially of a heart attack, five days before a crucial meeting of the Central Committee. A

---

23. *Ibid.*, p.79.

member of the Politburo, and a close friend of Stalin for many years, although by no means his puppet, Ordzhonikidze is said to have been concerned about Bukharin's fate and was incensed at the trial and sentence of Pyatakov who worked for him. He telephoned Yezhov, called him a 'filthy lickspittle' and demanded to see the documents in the case. He then telephoned Stalin and threatened that he would 'raise hell' about Bukharin's case if it was the last thing he did before he died, thus precipitating his own death sentence. Such was his standing in the Party that if he were to attempt to halt the purges and the trial of Bukharin he might not have been alone in the Central Committee and Stalin would have felt threatened.[24] On the other hand in the Plenum of the Central Committee held in February-March of 1937 it was Stalin alone who spoke against a trial or the death penalty for Bukharin although, with Ordzhonikidze's death only a few days before, his motives must be suspect.

In any event, it was not long after his telephone call to Stalin that NKVD officers arrived at Ordzhonikidze's flat with a search warrant and a few days later he was found shot, either by his own hand or that of another. Although he may have committed suicide under pressure, it is probable he was murdered since men were seen running

---

24. From the archives so far available there seems to be no evidence that Ordzhonikidze protested to the Central Committee against the use of terror against Party leaders. But, of course, he died before the vital meeting for this purpose took place. Cf. J. Arch Getty and Oleg V. Naumov. *The Road to Terror: Stalin and the Self-Destruction of the Bolsheviks, 1932-1939.* (New Haven, Yale University Press, 1999), p.283.

from his home immediately after the shooting. Whatever the truth, as with the death of Kirov once he was dead any opposition to Stalin that remained in the Politburo and Central Committee was a good deal weaker.

Subsequently, on 3 July 1937, Stalin sent a telegram to Yezhov and Party regional committees with instructions to set up three-man boards (Troikas) whose membership in each province was the Party First Secretary, an NKVD representative and the Procurator.[25] They were entirely extra-legal bodies who, as part of the Terror, were to prepare round-number quotas and target figures of persons to be executed or sent to the camps as anti-soviet elements, without charge or trial or even formal reference to articles of the penal code. The order involved the death and removal of whole unnamed sections of the population by numbers.

Pre-set quotas for arrests were given, for example, in an NKVD operational order headed, 'Concerning the punishment of former kulaks, criminals, and other anti-soviet elements' and dated 30 July 1937.[26] This set out 48 republics and regions across the USSR and against their names were listed over 200,000 first and second category numbers of citizens who were to be arrested by the troikas in each of the areas. Those most active were to be included in the first category and shot whilst those 'less hostile elements' included in the second category were to be sent

---

25. *Trud*. 88. 4 June 1992, 1, 4.
26. Document 170 in J. Arch Getty and Oleg V. Naumov. *The Road to Terror: Stalin and the Self-Destruction of the Bolsheviks, 1932-1939*. (New Haven, Yale University Press, 1999), pp.473-80.

to concentration camps or prison for a term ranging from eight to 10 years. Even more chilling, if that is possible, the order said that 'Families, members of which are *capable of* active anti-soviet actions ... are subject to being transferred to camps or labour settlements.'

Although it is sometimes argued that Stalin and his élite genuinely saw spies and enemies all around them, which is why they were not embarrassed at putting the records of their cruelties into the archives, this was a new Red Terror in a country that was not at war but was said to have achieved socialism. Not only countless victims were involved but under Stalin's direction their wives and children had also to be included in the lists that were drawn up. As Stalin privately told Georgi Dimitrov, head of the Comintern, in 1937,

Whoever tries to break the unity of the socialist state, whoever hopes to separate from it specific parts or nationalities, is a sworn enemy of the state, of the peoples of the USSR. And we will destroy any such enemy, even if he is an old Bolshevik, we will destroy his kin, his family. [We will destroy] anyone who by his actions or thoughts, yes even thoughts, encroaches on the unity of the socialist state.[27]

It is little wonder that Milovan Djilas in his *Conversations*

---

27. F.I. Firsov's archive notes from Dimitrov's diary. Quoted by J. Arch Getty. *The Politics of Repression Revisited.* In Chris Ward. ed. *The Stalinist Dictatorship.* (London, Arnold, 1998), p.121.

with Stalin wrote that 'Every crime was possible for Stalin, and there was not one he had not committed. Whatever standards we use to take his measure, he has the glory of being the greatest criminal in history – and, let us hope, for all time to come.'[28]

28. (Harmondsworth, Middlesex, Pelican Books, 1969), p.145.

CHAPTER 7

The Trial of Bukharin

The Military

By 1937 the Five-Year-Plans had to a large extent transformed the Soviet Union from a predominantly peasant society into an increasingly urban, industrial one. For some people it was a period of happy sacrifice and enthusiasm. For many others it meant misery with low wages, appalling housing conditions and severe shortages of food and other consumer goods. Above all, there was a pervasive atmosphere of suspicion and fear with the backcloth of slave labour, concentration camps, repression and death. And, despite the successes Stalin was determined to uproot and destroy those remaining leaders who believed there was a better way to build a socialist society.

In a portent of things to come, not only Bukharin but Marshal Nikolai Tukhachevsky also was mentioned by Radek in his trial. Although the context appeared to be innocent, and later in the trial Radek was to say that Tukhachevsky's attitude to the Party and the government was that of 'an absolutely devoted man', the required damage had been done and two months later the Marshal was dismissed as Chief of the General Staff. Within another month he, and other senior officers, were court martialled in June 1937 on charges of Trotskyism and treason to the Red Army and the peoples of the USSR. After being tortured mercilessly until they confessed, the accused were subjected to a secret trial lasting only one day and were promptly executed.[1] Tukhachevsky's wife became insane, his 11-year-old daughter and three of his sisters were sent to the Gulag and another sister and his two brothers were shot on Stalin's orders.

In the mayhem of the courts martial and the military slaughter that followed it the Soviet Union suffered the loss of three of its five marshals, almost all its top-ranking army commanders, 10 top naval officers, about two-thirds of the corps commanders, 60 per cent of divisional commanders and half of the brigade commanders. In addition, some tens of thousands of Party cadres in the army were also shot. The consequences were devastating in the war against Finland in 1939/40 and the early stages of the German invasion of the Soviet Union in the Second World War.

Yezhov Takes Over

In the course of the earlier trial of Zinoviev and his co-accused other important figures referred to as implicated in terror activities were Rykov and, as already

---

1. Years later analysis revealed bloodstains on Tukhachevsky's confession. *Isvestia*. (1989), 50.

mentioned, the still popular Bukharin. After the trial they were made the subject of the investigation Vyshinsky had threatened but, as there was not yet sufficient fabricated evidence available, and following opposition to extending the terror to Party leaders like themselves from Ordzhonikidze and others in the Politburo, this had been cancelled with an announcement from the state prosecutor's office on 10 September 1936 that no judicial basis for proceedings against them had been found. Stalin was not prepared to bow to such pressure for long, however, and, according to Khrushchev,[2] he and Zhdanov, whilst on holiday at the Black Sea, sent a telegram on 22 September to the Politburo claiming that the NKVD was four years behind in unmasking the traitors and that Yezhov must replace Yagoda as its head. This change-over occurred on 27 September and Yagoda was arrested at the beginning of April 1937. According to Nadezhda Mandelstam, Yagoda was now attacked in the press for having turned the forced-labour camps into rest homes, on which her husband, the poet Osip Mandelstam, ironically remarked 'I didn't know we were in the paws of such humanists.'[3]

To make it perfectly clear that Bukharin was not to be spared, in a speech delivered on 5 March 1937 Stalin said:

The present-day wreckers and diversionists, no matter

---

2.   *Secret Speech*. In *Khrushchev Remembers. Op. cit.*, p.575.
3.   Nadezhda Mandelstam. *Hope Against Hope: A Memoir*. (London, Collins & Harvill Press, 1971), p.9.

what disguise they adopt, whether Trotskyite or Bukharinite, have long ceased to represent a political trend in the labour movement; they have been transformed into a gang of professional wreckers, diversionists, spies and assassins devoid of principles and ideals. These gentlemen must of course be ruthlessly crushed and extirpated as enemies of the working class, as traitors to our country. That is clear and needs no further explanation.

Bukharin and Rykov were immediately expelled from the Party and the ball was now firmly in Vyshinsky's court.

The Culminating Trial

Bukharin's was the last of the show trials when he was brought to court, under article 58 of the criminal code, along with 20 others. These included Alexei Ivanovich Rykov, premier after Lenin and Politburo member, Genrikh Grigorievich Yagoda, former head of the NKVD, Nicolai Nikolaevich Krestinsky, a diplomat, and three prominent Kremlin doctors. Officially it was the 'Case of the Anti-Soviet Bloc of Rights and Trotskyites' tried before the Military Collegium of the Supreme Court of the USSR.[4] As usual in state trials, Ulrich was the presiding

---

4. Unless otherwise stated the quotations that follow are taken from the verbatim transcript of the trials. (Moscow, People's Commissariat of Justice of the USSR, 1938).

judge and Vyshinsky the chief prosecutor when the case opened on 2 March 1938. The charges were similar to those in the preceding show trials and, in addition to being responsible for the assassination of Kirov, they were accused of causing the death of Kuibyshev, and poisoning Maxim Gorky and his son and the former OGPU chief, Menzhinsky. So far as Bukharin is concerned he was also charged with having attempted to murder Lenin and Stalin in 1918. The report of the preliminary investigation occupied some 50 volumes which lay on a table in the courtroom during the trial but were not published or made available for research until the archives were recently opened.

Bukharin had been the leader of the 'Left Communists' in the period immediately following the October Revolution but after the death of Lenin he became the spokesman of the moderate, right wing of the Party advocating a non-violent transition to socialism, and is credited with originating the doctrine of 'socialism in one country'. He had opposed the Left Opposition of Trotsky and strongly defended the policy of the NEP and came to consider the forced industrialization and collectivization imposed by Stalin to be disastrous and a betrayal of the Revolution. Moreover, at the Seventeenth Party Congress in 1934 he had made an impassioned speech warning of the danger of Hitler whilst Stalin was telling the delegates 'Of course we are far from enthusiastic about the fascist regime in Germany. But fascism is beside the point, if only because fascism in Italy, for example, has not kept the USSR from establishing the best of relations with that country.'[5] By 1938 Stalin had been obliged to change his tune but that only encouraged him to accuse Bukharin of conspiring with the Nazis against the Soviet Union.

Fantasy

Once the trial had commenced Vyshinsky, in an endeavour to make Bukharin feel trapped, questioned other defendants first. But the fantasy aspect of the trial was soon revealed in an exchange between Vyshinsky and one of the accused, Isaak Zelensky, who had been the chief of a consumers' co-operative network:

Vyshinsky: Were there cases when your organization connected with the butter business threw glass into the butter?

Zelensky: There were cases when glass was found in butter.

Vyshinsky: Glass was not 'found', but thrown into the butter. You understand the difference: thrown into the butter. Were there such cases, or not?

Zelensky: There were cases when glass was thrown into the butter.

Vyshinsky: Were there cases when your accomplices, fellow participators in the criminal plot against the Soviet power and the Soviet people threw nails into the butter?

Zelensky: There were.

---

5.   Report of the Congress. *Op. cit.,* pp.13-14.

Vyshinsky: For what purpose? To make it 'tastier'?
Zelensky: That is clear.

A little later:

Vyshinsky: That is, the public was offered felt boots in the summer and summer shoes in the winter?
Zelensky: Yes.

Equally bizarre was the evidence given of Yagoda attempting to have Yezhov poisoned with a spray gun.

All the accused pleaded guilty except Krestinsky who caused a sensation in court when he told Ulrich: 'I plead not guilty. I am not a Trotskyite. I was never a member of the bloc of Rights and Trotskyites, of whose existence I was not aware. Nor have I committed any of the crimes with which I personally am charged, in particular I plead not guilty to the charge of having connections with German intelligence services.' Questioned by Vyshinsky, one of the accused, S.A. Bessonov, stated on cue that he had been involved with Krestinsky in Trotskyite plots. This was denied by Krestinsky and Vyshinsky then turned to him to ask about his confession during interrogation.

Vyshinsky: But what about your admission?
Krestinsky: During the investigation I gave false testimony several times.
Vyshinsky: You said: 'I did not formally belong to the Trotskyite centre.' Is that true or not?
Krestinsky: I did not belong to it at all.
Vyshinsky: You say that formally you did not belong. What is true and what is not true here? Perhaps it is all

true, or it is all untrue, or only half of it is true?
What percentage, how many grams of it are true?

Krestinsky: I did not belong to the Trotskyite centre because I was not a Trotskyite.

Shortly afterwards, speaking of his pre-trial interrogation by Vyshinsky, Krestinsky added that he had deliberately confirmed his earlier testimony.

Vyshinsky: You deliberately confirmed it. You were misleading the Prosecutor. Is that so, or not?

Krestinsky: No.

Vyshinsky: Why did you have to mislead me?

Krestinsky: I simply considered that if I were to say what I am saying today – that it was not in accordance with the facts – my declaration would not reach the leaders of the Party and the Government.

In other words, he had 'confessed' at the preliminary investigation in order to appear in open court where he could publicly deny his guilt. He was under no illusion as to what would have happened to him if he had not done so. However, later in the trial, in the face of allegations from his co-accused, who had failed to follow his example, and after having spent a night in the hands of the NKVD, Krestinsky was finally brought to say that he was guilty of treason and treachery.

Rykov, in giving his evidence, admitted taking part in the formation of an illegal organization but denied involvement in particular crimes. Nevertheless, although he had been expelled from the Politburo with Bukharin in 1929, he now turned on his former friend and colleague.

Bukharin had told him, he said, that he had had connections with a terrorist named Semyonov ever since the Socialist Revolutionaries had attempted to assassinate Lenin.

When at one stage Yagoda protested that he was telling the truth and Vyshinsky asked him why then he lied at the preliminary investigation he replied with fury, 'I told you. Permit me not to reply to this question.' When Ulrich intervened, an American observer at the trial noted that Yagoda turned on him and said 'You can drive me, but not too far. I'll say what I want to say ... but ... do not drive me too far.'[6] As the former head of the NKVD, Yagoda was the repository of many vital secrets about both that agency and the earlier show trials and this must have been a cause of concern to Stalin and Vyshinsky, particularly as he had clearly had some involvement in the assassination of Kirov. However, having already incredibly admitted to planning to seize the Kremlin, murdering his predecessor, Menzhinsky, as well as Maxim Gorky and his son, and Kuibyshev, he henceforth held his peace.

Bukharin's Defiance

Bukharin, who had worked with Lenin in his European exile, unlike Vyshinsky who joined the Bolshevik Party

---

6. This response is not in the official transcript, which was edited, but was reported by Walter Duranty, who was in the court. See his *Kremlin and the People.* (London, Hamish Hamilton, 1942), pp.84-5.

only in 1920, had the highest stature in the Party of all those accused in the three show trials. As such his influence posed the greatest threat to Stalin's personality cult and policies. To secure his participation in the trial he was made to suffer three months of interrogation during which threats were made about his young wife Anna Larina and their infant child as well as his previous wife and their 13-year-old daughter, Svetlana. As a result, and perhaps hoping to send coded messages about the Terror to those prepared to listen, he accepted general responsibility under his Indictment but he refused to admit being involved in the direct actions alleged in the criminal charges against him or of planning the death of Lenin. He also denied being concerned in talks about weakening the Soviet state or accelerating wrecking activities. At one point Ulrich pointedly told him that he was beating about the bush and not dealing with the crimes. And Vyshinsky accused the alleged conspirators of being a 'gang of murderers, spies, diversionists and wreckers'. To which Bukharin replied that in order to be a gang the members must know each other and he had never met or heard of five of his fellow 'conspirators'. He further said Vyshinsky's logic was tautology, that is, the acceptance of what is yet to be proved as already proven. Indeed, in all Soviet trials there was a presumption of guilt, not the 'bourgeois' presumption of innocence.

Bukharin testified that he did not know if Kirov was assassinated on instructions from the 'bloc of Rights and Trotskyites'.When Vyshinsky turned to Rykov to put the same point Rykov also denied any knowledge of involvement by the 'bloc'. Yagoda, however, admitted giving instructions to the NKVD in Leningrad not to place obstacles in the way of the assassination. But at that time he was very close to Stalin and busy attacking Bukharin and Rykov.

In totally denying espionage, a charge not made in his preliminary examination but sprung on him in court, Bukharin declared that the two accused who had testified against him about espionage were *agents provocateurs*. When Vyshinsky nevertheless told him that all the material of the investigation showed him to be a spy for an intelligence service the following exchange took place:

Bukharin: During the year I spent in prison I was not once asked about it.

Vyshinsky: We are asking you here in an open proletarian court, we are asking you here in this court before the whole world.

Bukharin: But you did not ask me this before.

Vyshinsky: I am asking you again, on the basis of the testimony which was here given against you; do you choose to admit before the Soviet Court by what intelligence service you were enlisted – the British, German or Japanese?

Bukharin: None.

Vyshinsky: I have no more questions to put to Bukharin.

Smarting from this setback and Bukharin's general defiance, Vyshinsky later venomously declared that 'The hypocrisy and perfidy of this man exceeds the most perfidious and monstrous crimes known to the history of mankind.' Speaking of history, at one point Bukharin was saying 'It must be said for the sake of historical exactitude ...' when Vyshinsky interrupted him to say 'Don't trouble to speak for history, accused Bukharin. History will itself record what will be interesting for history.' And so it was to prove.

'Plan to Assassinate Lenin'

Towards the end of the trial Vyshinsky brought forward the allegation that Bukharin had planned the assassination of Lenin and Stalin in 1918; the charge Bukharin was most determined to refute. Briefly, what had happened was as follows. In 1918 Bukharin, with many others, opposed the Brest-Litovsk peace treaty with Germany for which Lenin had great difficulty in obtaining the support of the Party's Central Committee. After all, the Party line had hitherto been that the Revolution should be spread to Germany and the rest of Europe through the war. In alliance with the Bolsheviks in government at the time were the Left Socialist Revolutionaries who were also against signing the treaty. They wished to join with the Bolshevik opponents to form an alternative government and continue to wage a revolutionary war. Apart from this problem Lenin faced he kept the negotiations with the Germans secret from the elected Soviets thus explicitly asserting the right of the Party and not the Soviets to make policy.[7]

In the end the Left Socialist Revolutionaries made approaches to Bukharin and Pyatakov to arrest Lenin for 24 hours, declare war on Germany and then put Lenin back in office to carry on the war. Lenin is said to have laughed aloud when told of the idea. In any event, nothing came of it and when the Left Socialist Revolutionaries on their own allegedly instigated a coup against the Bolsheviks in July 1918 Lenin had their Party dissolved.[8] He did not, however, bear any grudge against Bukharin and Pyatakov who remained in the leadership of the Bolshevik Party. Bukharin openly published the facts about the incident in *Pravda* on 3 January 1924 and they were repeated in subsequent histories of the Party until Stalin laid out his revised, and henceforth only, history in 1938.

Vyshinsky called five witnesses to support his charge of attempted assassination. But they were already being prosecuted separately and may well have received inducements to procure their evidence against Bukharin. When Bukharin started to put questions to them they were ruled to be out of order by both Vyshinsky and Ulrich. An example of the means taken to prevent Bukharin's questioning is revealed in the following excerpt from the transcript of the trial about the alleged plot between the Left Communists, including Bukharin, and the Left

---

7.   Jane Burbank. *Lenin and the Law in Revolutionary Russia. Slavic Review*, vol.54.1. (Cambridge, Mass. American Association for the Advancement of Slavic Studies. Spring 1995), p.41.

8.   See Katkov. *Op. cit.*, pp.172-75.

Socialist Revolutionaries to kill Lenin:

Bukharin: I wish to ask whether the witness Yakovleva was aware that Kuibyshev, Menzhinsky and Yaroslavsky belonged to the 'Left Communists'?

Vyshinsky: I ask this question to be ruled out as having no bearing on the case.

The President: You need not answer this question, as it has no bearing on the case.

Bukharin: Then I ask Citizen the President to explain to me whether I have the right to put such questions as I wish, or whether my questions are determined by Citizen the Procurator.

The President: Accused Bukharin, Yakovleva was called here to give testimony as to your anti-Soviet activity, the activity of Nikolai Ivanovich Bukharin. In connection with her testimony you wished to put several questions to her in relation to matters concerning you, and not any other persons.

Bukharin: Quite so, but I ask for an explanation from Citizen the President as to whether I have the right to put such questions as I consider necessary to put, or whether their character is determined by someone else, particularly, by Citizen the Procurator.

The President: You put one question and received a reply to it. Do you still wish to put questions?

Bukharin: Yes, very much so.

Vyshinsky: Allow me to make the following remark: I consider it necessary to explain Article 257 of the Code of Criminal Procedure, which defines, firstly, that the President guides the Court investigation, and, secondly, that at the Court

	investigation the President rules out of the Court investigation and the speeches for the prosecution and the defence all points that have no bearing on the case under trial.
Bukharin:	Then, Citizen Procurator, I ask for an explanation ...
The President:	Citizen the Procurator will give you no explanation.
Bukharin:	Then I ask Citizen the President of the Court to explain to me whether the question of the composition of the central group of the 'Left Communists' has any bearing on the case or not?
The President:	I completely rule out your question ...
Bukharin:	I still have a number of questions.

At this point, at Vyshinsky's request, the president read out the words of Article 257 and Bukharin again indicated that he wished to ask further questions.

Bukharin:	I ask witness Yakovleva to say whether she denies that in the Central Committee prior to the Brest-Litovsk Peace the majority of the votes was held by the 'Left Communists' plus the Trotskyites.
The President:	What bearing has this on your criminal role?
Bukharin:	It has this much bearing, that I wish thereby to motivate and explain the point that it was absolutely senseless to strive for a plot ...
The President:	The Court is interested in your role in the plot against the leaders of the Soviet government, and this is now the subject of the testimony.
Bukharin:	Good, then allow me to put the following question. Does witness Yakovleva deny that the

'Left Communists' prior to the Party Congress strove to receive a majority in the Party by legal means?

The President: The question has nothing whatever to do with the charge preferred against you of organizing a plot against the Soviet power, and therefore I rule it irrelevant.

Bukharin: Does Yakovleva deny that I was one of the members of the Presidium of the Congress in Moscow, one of the members of the Presidium which at the time of the murder of Mirbach (the German ambassador) arrested the faction of 'Left' Socialist- Revolutionaries?

The President: This question has no bearing whatsoever on your criminal activity. I rule it irrelevant.

Bukharin: Does witness Yakovleva deny that in 1919 I was wounded at a meeting of the Moscow Committee by a 'Left' Socialist-Revolutionary bomb?

The President: This question has nothing whatever to do with the charge against you of being concerned in a plot. I rule this question irrelevant also.

Bukharin: I have no more questions.

Not only was Bukharin ground down by the refusal to allow him to question the witness in this ritualistic approach to procedure when his life was at stake, but the exchanges also reveal clearly how the President of the court did not mind it being seen that he considered him to be guilty.

Towards the end of the trial Vyshinsky demanded that 'the traitors and spies who were selling our country must be shot like dirty dogs! Our people are demanding one thing: crush the accursed reptiles! Time will pass. The graves of the hateful traitors will grow over with weeds and thistles ... Over the road cleared of the last scum and filth of the past, we, our people, with our beloved leader and teacher, the great Stalin, at our head will march as before onwards and onwards, towards Communism!'

Medieval Jurisprudence

Bukharin, in his final speech to the court (and the world) said 'I plead guilty to ... the sum total of crimes committed by this counter-revolutionary organization' and then negated that statement by adding, 'irrespective of whether or not I knew of, or whether or not I took a direct part in, any particular act.' And discrediting his whole 'confession' he devastatingly remarked, 'The confession of the accused is a medieval principle of jurisprudence.'

The British diplomat, Fitzroy Maclean, who attended the trial, described Bukharin in making his final speech as standing 'frail and defiant' and, whilst admitting in general the case against him, proceeding 'to tear it to bits, while Vyshinsky, powerless to intervene, sat uneasily in his place, looking embarrassed and yawning ostentatiously.'[9]

At 4 a.m. on 13 March, Ulrich pronounced the death penalty for 18 of the accused with Pletnev receiving 25 years in prison, Rakovsky 20 years and Bessonov 15 years. Two days later, Bukharin, Rykov and the others were shot.

---

9.   *Escape to Adventure*. (Boston, Little, Brown, 1950), p.74.

In his last letter to Stalin on 10 December 1937, Bukharin wrote, 'Standing on the edge of a precipe, from which there is no return, I tell you on my word of honour, as I await my death, that I am innocent of those crimes which I admitted to at the investigation.'[10]

After all the arrests, trials and executions of Party leaders, diplomats, soldiers and so on, it must have been difficult for those Russians who believed in Stalin not to think that from the Revolution onwards Soviet society had been largely run by traitors and foreign agents.

Bukharin's Testament

Previously, on the day of his arrest and knowing he was soon to die, Bukharin had dictated to his wife, Anna Larina, a letter which he implored her to memorize for a future generation. In it he denied all the criminal charges against him and urged her to raise their young son as a Bolshevik. Silently reciting it 'like a prayer' throughout her 20 years captivity in the Gulag she did memorize it and was eventually able to publish it in 1988 during Mikhail Gorbachov's glasnost.

Earlier, and before all the investigations were carried out, Khrushchev had declared in his secret speech that 'when the cases of some of these so-called "spies" and "saboteurs" were examined, it was found that all their cases were fabricated.' Adding, 'Many thousands of honest

---

10. Document 198. Getty and Naumov. *Op. cit.,* p.556.

and innocent Communists have died as a result of this monstrous falsification of such "cases", as a result of the fact that all kinds of slanderous "confessions" were accepted, and as a result of the practice of forcing accusations against oneself and others.'[11] Thus did history, which Vyshinsky had derided, vindicate Bukharin and reveal the core of the show trials to be works of fiction.

At the beginning of his letter Bukharin declared, 'I am helpless before an infernal machine that seems to use medieval methods, yet possesses gigantic power, fabricates organized slander, acts boldly and confidently.' The NKVD was 'a degenerate organization of unprincipled, dissolute, well-kept functionaries who, enjoying the former authority of the Cheka, seeking to satisfy the pathological suspiciousness of Stalin (I fear to say more), pursuing rank and glory, perform their foul deeds without, incidentally, understanding that they are simultaneously destroying themselves: history does not tolerate the witnesses to dirty deeds!'

After saying that his head alone, guilty of nothing, would implicate thousands more of the innocent, Bukharin's letter ends with the words:

I turn to you, the future generation of Party leaders, on whom will fall the historic mission of clearing the monstrous cloud of crimes that in these terrible days is growing more and more grandiose, spreading like wildfire and smothering the Party.

---

11. *Secret Speech. Op. cit.*, p.583.

I address myself to all Party members!

In what may be the final days of my life, I am certain that sooner or later the filter of history will inevitably wash the filth from my head.

I never was a traitor; I would have unhesitatingly traded my own life for Lenin's. I loved Kirov and never undertook anything against Stalin.

I ask the new, young, and honest generation of Party leaders to read my letter aloud at a plenum of the Central Committee, to vindicate me, and to reinstate me in the Party.

Know, comrades, that the banner you bear in a triumphant march toward communism contains a drop of my blood, too.[12]

In the meantime Stalin's Terror had made him the unassailable autocrat with a virtual monopoly of political power in a system in which law existed only in name and millions of people were destroyed for spurious reasons on the basis that every activity was subordinate to the aims of the state. And in the end, apart from the figures given by Khrushchev in his secret speech of the decimation of the top leaders of Stalin's own Party, over one million people who had been Party members in 1935 were executed, or died in the Gulag camps such as Kolyma and Vorkuta in the frozen territories of the Arctic.

---

12. Anna Larina Bukharin. *This I Cannot Forget: The Memoirs of Nicolai Bukharin's Widow.* (London, Hutchinson, 1993), pp.344-5.

CHAPTER 8

Law as a Façade for Terror

Coercion and Consent

Far from the tyranny and terror abating with the proclaimed achievement in 1936 of socialism and a society free from class struggle it was intensified with capitalist encirclement taking the blame. During 1937 the pay scale of NKVD personnel was roughly quadrupled and became higher than that of any other government agency. They were also given the best living accommodation, rest homes and hospitals and were awarded medals and decorations for successful work. Heavy recruitment meant their numbers increased to hundreds of thousands and they became an army with military titles and spy units known as special sections located in all schools, factories, tenements and major enterprises. Dossiers were kept on tens of millions of people.[1] Untold numbers were tortured, held in prisons and the Gulag and killed, although this was hidden from the remainder of the population as far as possible and was barely mentioned in the press.

Nevertheless, security police were formally required to

---

1.   R. Medvedev. *Let History Judge. Op. cit.*, pp.657-8.

obtain the permission of procurators before making arrests. Since procurators were as liable to arrest as anyone else (particularly for lack of zeal in the Terror) this led to the rubber-stamping of arrest orders and providing the police with signed blank arrest forms. If a police officer forgot to obtain permission for an arrest most procurators provided back-dated orders.[2]

At the same time, since enthusiasm for work and hope for the future had to be maintained, Stalin and the media were telling the people that it was a joy to live in a socialist society. Under continuous bombardment from all sections of the media millions of people quarantined from the truth, both of what was happening in their own country and about life outside Russia, did believe that they were enjoying a good life. Indeed many of them were, particularly some industrial workers who were not interested in internationalism and the upwardly mobile who moved into management and the bureaucracy in a society where those they replaced had disappeared. This gave Stalin's revolutionary process its popular support from below, although despite having Russian vitality millions of people had to bear their creative abilities being stunted and unused.

Despite his 'liberalism' Bukharin had been a strong supporter of the Cheka and its activities, but that was in the period of the civil war and War Communism. Even at that time, however, although fully aware of the coercive role of the state machine he was able to extend the

---

2. *Ibid.,* p.393.

Leninist view of the state to incorporate the need of the dominant bourgeois class to take account of the importance of ideology in also securing control of the people by consent given that force alone is not a sufficient basis for a political system. In the *ABC of Communism*, written with E. Preobrazhensky in 1919, he explained that 'The bourgeoisie is well aware that it cannot control the working masses by the use of force alone. It is necessary that the workers' brains should be completely enmeshed as if in a spider's web. The bourgeois state looks upon the workers as working cattle; these beasts must labour but they must not bite ... the capitalist state maintains specialists to stupefy and subdue the proletariat; it maintains bourgeois teachers and professors, the clergy, bourgeois authors and journalists.'[3] If the words bourgeoisie, bourgeois and capitalist are replaced with communist and socialist, and the clergy deleted, this statement would be entirely appropriate to describe the non-coercive aspect of Stalin's rule. The new 1936 Constitution, and the propaganda surrounding it, were meant to be seen as part of that aspect.

The Stalin Constitution

Whilst the Moscow show trials were in progress, and Stalin was attempting through his foreign minister, Maxim Litvinov, to achieve collective security with the

---

3.   (London, The Communist Party of Great Britain, 1922), p.44.

West European countries against Hitler and his allies, the year 1936 saw the introduction of the Stalin Constitution.[4] This replaced the Congress of Soviets and the Central Executive Committee with a Supreme Soviet having two chambers, one for the Union and another for nationalities. And for the first time in Russia a Constitution confirmed the supremacy of the Communist Party, although this meant the supremacy of Stalin since Party bodies were meeting less and less frequently and in any event were totally under his control. However, in other respects the Constitution was intended to convey the message that the regime was socialist and democratic.

The Party, said Stalin in introducing it, provided 'democracy for the working people, that is, democracy for all … That is why I think that the Constitution of the USSR is the only thoroughly democratic Constitution in the world.'[5] And, indeed, against a background of fear of the growing threat of fascism, it was well received in many parts of the world. However, Stalin's claim was clearly not the true state of affairs in the midst of the Great Terror, in which seven to eight million people were arrested of whom about three million were shot or died and the camps swelled to nine million inmates,[6] and when the Party was self-perpetuating, all-powerful and unwilling to permit dissent. Nor was it ever to be so.

---

4. The 1936 Constitution. (Moscow, Foreign Languages Publishing House, 1950).
5. *Ibid.*
6. Stephen F. Cohen. *Bukharin and the Bolshevik Revolution: A Political Biography 1888-1938.* (Oxford, Oxford University Press, 1980), pp.340/1.

The drafting committee had included Stalin, and also Bukharin, Rykov and Radek on each of whom he was soon to pounce. Many of its articles bear the imprint of Bukharin and its democratic features (utopian in Stalin's Russia) were probably inspired by him, although its freedoms were granted only, it said in a revealing phrase, 'in order to strengthen socialist society' and availed nothing when Bukharin, Rykov and Radek were brought to trial.

In any event, it was too good to be true and Stalin accepted it, and the credit for it, partly as a façade for the Terror and also secure in the knowledge that he never had the slightest intention of giving effect to it. It can be compared with chapter 7 of the more likely to be observed post-Stalin Constitution of 1977 setting out similar 'Basic Rights, Freedoms and Duties of Citizens' to those of 1936.[7] Here there was added a clause which read 'Enjoyment by citizens of their rights and freedoms must not be to the detriment of the interests of society or the state, or infringe the rights of other citizens.'[8] In 1936 such a clause would have been superfluous.

In any event there was no procedure by which the individual citizen could enforce the illusory freedoms of speech, press and assembly the Constitution 'guaranteed', despite Stalin's assertion to the contrary.[9] And in the first 'elections' under the Constitution, held in December 1937,

---

7. (Moscow, Novosti Press Agency Publishing House, 1978), p.40.
8. *Ibid.*
9. J. Stalin. *Problems of Leninism. Op. cit.*, p.692.

all the Party-approved candidates were unopposed (contrary to the original idea for the Constitution) and together they received 99.4 per cent of the votes cast. In defending a one-party state Stalin said that parties represented classes in society and classes had disappeared. Not that he was prepared to tolerate more than one party before they had apparently melted away.

Law Strengthened

As far as the law is concerned, article 14 of the Constitution called for 'legislation concerning the judicial system and judicial procedure, with criminal and civil codes to replace the existing republican codes.' With this the original Bolshevik concept of dispensing with the law was finally put on the back burner. Instead, the law was now to be strengthened following Stalin's speech on the draft of the new Constitution in which he said, 'we need stability of laws now more than ever.'[10] 'Revolutionary legality' was in future to involve strict observance of the laws except by the Party leadership and the NKVD, which was nothing new. However, all-union codes were never adopted while Stalin lived despite several drafts being prepared. The problem was the gap between his desire on the one hand for stable laws and his arbitrary use of terror on the other. In any event, the Supreme Court remained

---

10. J. Stalin. *On the Draft Constitution of the USSR (1936)*. (Moscow, Foreign Languages Publishing House, 1950), p.58.

subordinate to the government and the Party which retained their judicial, legislative and executive powers which Lenin had said they should have.

By article 111 of the Constitution an accused person on trial had 'the right to be defended by counsel', a 'right' that proved not only to be largely illusory during the Terror but of little value even when exercised. Article 112 provided that 'Judges are independent and subject only to the law'. But the law expressed the policy of the Party and thus their independence from that policy was a chimera. The Soviet jurist, N.N. Polyansky, put it this way in 1950:

The independence of the judges referred to in article 112 of the Stalin Constitution does not and cannot signify their independence of politics. The judges are subject only to the law – this provision expresses the subordination of the judges to the policy of the Soviet regime which finds its expression in the law.

The demand that the work of the judge be subject to the law and the demand that it be subject to the policy of the Communist Party cannot be in contradiction in our country.[11]

Although it did not say so directly, the Constitution implied that Soviet law was socialist law. Accordingly, the theory that it would wither away was now buried, as was Pashukanis. On 20 January 1937 *Pravda* announced that he was an 'enemy of the people' and that he and his

---

11. Quoted by Merle Fainsod. *How Russia is Ruled. Op. cit.,* p.375.

followers were wreckers. They were promptly arrested and Pashukanis died in prison later that year. Nicolai Krylenko, a loyal servant of Stalin but also a public critic of Vyshinsky, was also arrested and was shot the following year. Pashukanis's replacement was the same Vyshinsky, whose acts and violent courtroom speeches already noticed had introduced a new form of terror into the legal system. And on the Constitution also Vyshinsky was carried away by his own rhetoric. The Soviet Union, he was to say, was 'the land of Socialism, the land of genuine popular rule, of genuine democracy, a true, consistent and fearless defender of the democratic rights and liberties of the peoples ...'[12]

Jurist Traitors

In 1938 Vyshinsky gave an address to a Congress in Moscow on *Problems of the Sciences of Soviet State and Law*. It was filled with vituperation against former colleagues as well as abundant quotations from Stalin 'the mightiest genius who carried on the work of Marx, Engels and Lenin'. In it he said 'Over a series of years a position almost of monopoly in legal science has been occupied by a group of persons who have turned out to be provocateurs and traitors – people who knew how actually to contrive the work of betraying our science, our state, and our

---

12. Andrei Y. Vyshinsky. *The Teaching of Lenin and Stalin on Proletarian Revolution and the State*. (London, Soviet News, 1948), p.120.

fatherland under the mask of defending Marxism-Leninism.' Moreover, 'these persons strove to dash from the hands of the proletariat and the toilers of our land the Marx-Lenin doctrine of law and state which proved to be so potent an instrument in the struggle with the many bestial foes of socialism.' As a consequence, 'the legal-science front still continues to lag behind the demands of our epoch – behind the demands of the Party and of the government.'[13]

Following Stalin's pronouncements, said Vyshinsky, the law had to be strengthened because 'it reinforces the stability of the state order and of the state discipline, and multiplies tenfold the powers of socialism, mobilizing and directing them against forces hostile to them.'[14] As with other spheres, an alarming number of jurists and prosecutors were imprisoned and killed, since, in Vyshinsky's view, they and their theories served the class enemy and it followed as a matter of course that they were traitors.

An attack on the 'wrecker Trotsky-Bukharin' theories of law of Pashukanis, Krylenko and others appeared in the Party journal *Bolshevik* on 1 September 1937 under the title *Socialism and Law*.[15] Signed by 'P. Yudin', a hardline Marxist historian and not a lawyer, it was filled with quotations from Marx, Engels, Lenin and Stalin and bore

---

13. Hugh W. Babb. *Soviet Legal Philosophy. Op. cit.*, pp.303-4, 313.
14. Andrei Y. Vyshinksy. *The Law of the Soviet State.* (New York, The Macmillan Company, 1948), p.51.
15. No.17, pp.31-46. Reproduced in Babb. *Soviet Legal Philosophy. Op. cit.*, pp.281-301.

the hallmarks of Vyshinsky's vitriolic style against so-called pseudo-specialists in law. Such 'jurists' had preached that Soviet law had borrowed from bourgeois law and was bourgeois in form. On the contrary, Yudin said, the content defined the form and the Stalin Constitution had crowned the struggle to construct a system of the socialist legal order. Far from the law withering away socialist law had to be developed systematically in order to safeguard socialist property and the rules of socialist community living. 'In the struggles with the survivals of capitalism – with addle-pated foes of the people, the adherents of Trotsky and Bukharin, and the fascist agents of Germany and Japan – the socialist state rests on the support of the entire people. Socialist law is the mighty instrumentality which will even further deal death to all the foes of socialism.'

Vyshinsky's 'Law'

Vyshinsky had long opposed the 'nihilist' view of Soviet law advocated by Krylenko, Stuchka and Pashukanis in favour of a professional legal system, and a new generation of jurists and prosecutors were now to be trained in the spirit of his attempt to produce a theory of lasting socialist law, and to ensure that the law was used as a hammer against enemies – for the most part imaginary. Until this time most Soviet investigators, procurators and judges had little if any legal education or experience[16] and it would still take some years to train them. Indeed, many of them lost their jobs and were arrested in the Party purges and the Terror, sometimes with reason when procurators rubber-stamped indictments without even reading them.

According to Peter Solomon Jr. 'As of early 1938, 51.4 per cent of judges in the Kazakh republic were new; half those in the Turkmen republic had less than a year's experience; and in one *raion* (district) of Moscow only one of eight judges in place in June 1938 antedated the spring of 1937.'[17] Even the Supreme Court of the USSR was subjected to a severe purge in the spring of 1938 and did not sit until new judges were appointed in the autumn. What effect the inevitable worry and fear must have had on the judicial capacity of procurators and judges can only be imagined.

Law, Vyshinsky claimed in defiance of Marx, Engels and Lenin, did not reach its fullest expression under capitalism but in socialist society. But he had in mind more than the widely accepted view of law as the sum of the general rules of behaviour enforced by the state. He realised the importance of law as legitimating device in Soviet society and endeavoured to remystify it after it had been left exposed by Krylenko and the early legal nihilists

---

16. See Peter H. Solomon Jr. *Soviet Criminal Justice and the Great Terror.* (*Slavic Review*. 46, American Association for the Advancement of Slavic Studies, Inc. 1987), p.393.
17. *Ibid.,* p.401.

as a naked weapon of state control.[18] His definition of law was:

> the totality (a) of the rules of conduct, expressing the will of the dominant class and established in legal order, and (b) of customs and rules of community life sanctioned by state authority – their application being guaranteed by the compulsive force of the state in order to guard, secure, and develop social relationships and social orders advantageous and agreeable to the dominant class.

Soviet law, in contrast, was:

> the aggregate of the rules of conduct established in the form of legislation by the authority of the toilers and expressive of their will. The effective operation of these rules is guaranteed by the entire coercive force of the socialist state in order to defend, to secure, and to develop relationships and arrangements advantageous and agreeable to the toilers, and completely and finally to annihilate capitalism and its remnants in the economic system, the way of life, and human consciousness – in order to build a communist society.[19]

The effect of this is, as Professor Hans Kelsen has pointed

---

18. Eugene Huskey. *Vyshinskii, Krylenko, and the Shaping of the Soviet Legal Order. (Slavic Review. Ibid.),* p.416.
19. *Ibid.,* p.50.

out, that 'since soviet law does not fall under the concept of "law" as defined by Vyshinsky, the so-called soviet law is neither bourgeois nor socialist law: it is no law at all.'[20]

In any event, if there are no antagonistic classes left and law is expressive of the will of all the people it would not need to be coercive. Furthermore, nothing was said about the rule of law because this never operated in the Soviet Union. The doctrine of the rule of law means that all persons are judged in ordinary courts and will not be punished except for a breach of the ordinary law which is fixed and made public. It also ensures that laws and courts do not have extraordinary status and that arbitrary power is not exercised. In the Soviet Union, simply because a 'law' was decreed by the state or by the Party or Stalin it was *ipso facto* legitimate, much as was the case with the Nazis and Hitler in Germany and, of course, a number of other dictatorships.

The lengthy book, *The Law of the Soviet State*,[21] in which Vyshinsky set out the new dogma of law was published in the Soviet Union in 1936 and was required reading not only for jurists but also for state administrators and Soviet students of government. In its core its definition of Soviet law was not so different from Stuchka's two decades earlier, but its elaborations formed the basis of the law for the terror trials in which Vyshinsky played such a prominent part.

But the feared prosecutor had another side to him. In

20. Kelsen. *Op. cit.*, p.132.
21. *Op. cit.*

his *Soviet Legal Philosophy* he fawned on his master with phrases such as 'the great Stalin',[22] 'the mightiest genius who carried on the work of Marx, Engels and Lenin: Stalin.'[23] And, 'a genius in scholarship and in the Marxist theory.'[24] On Lenin and Stalin, he said that 'they defined the direction of the policy of the soviet state – having illuminated the lines of that direction with a genius' prevision of the future and with a genius' penetration – raising before the soviet people the curtain of the future and illuminating the course of events in the years to come.'[25]

Yet in spite of his prominence and power this feared Soviet scourge of defendants knew his place and must also have been fearful himself of the tyrant behind his elbow. Perhaps he remembered the fate, recounted graphically by Solzhenitsyn, of the factory director who was arrested and sent to the camps for 10 years after being the first to stop applauding Stalin's name at a conference![26]

Vyshinsky closely linked himself with Stalin's theses of the intensification of the class struggle under socialism and that the ultimate withering away of the state would occur only through a strengthening of state power. It is difficult to square these with Stalin's assertion in his speech on the Constitution that antagonistic classes no longer existed in the Soviet Union, although he did refer

---

22. *Soviet Legal Philosophy. Op. cit.,* p.304.
23. *Ibid.,* p.305.
24. *Ibid.,* p.429.
25. *Ibid.,* p.430.
26. *The Gulag Archipelago. Op. cit.,* pp.69/70.

to continued foreign encirclement.

The Great Terror Subsides

In 1937 the maximum duration of deprivation of freedom was extended from 10 years to 25 years.[27] Nevertheless, within a year some subtle changes taking place could be discerned. With the country dislocated and industry declining, under Beria, who replaced Yezhov at the end of 1938, the mass purges began to subside. This was perhaps inevitable since many millions of people had 'disappeared' and as Zhdanov, who had taken part in the Terror, complained the low quality and poor education of the new Party leaders promoted as a result of the purges was causing problems.[28] Extraordinary laws and extrajudicial organs were now somewhat restrained, unjustified prosecutions began to decline and the regular courts and laws played a greater role and helped place limits on the terror.[29] The Supreme Court required strict standards of evidence in criminal trials and re-established review by appeal. But the system of state repression remained. Even Vyshinsky made some attempt in 1939 to control the

---

27. SZ (1937). 66/297.
28. Getty and Manning. *Stalinist Terror: New Perspectives.* (Cambridge, Cambridge University Press, 1993), pp.36-37.
29. Oleg V. Khlevniuk. *The Politburo, Penal Policy, and 'Legal Reforms' in the 1930s.* In Peter H. Solomon, Jr. *Reforming Justice in Russia, 1864-1996: Power, Culture and the Limits of Legal Order.* (New York. M.E. Sharpe, 1997), p.203.

procedures of the Troikas, although this was no doubt in order to advance his own interests and the power of the Procuracy. Nevertheless, on 14 June 1939 the President of the Military Collegium of the Supreme Court, V. Ulrich, wrote to Stalin *asking for instructions* on when to allow attorneys for the defence to have access to court records. He considered it advisable, as a rule, not to allow them where it might divulge the methods employed in preliminary investigations or the names of people not yet arrested. He thought it would be right to allow defence attorneys after two or three months, but he still needed instructions from Stalin.[30]

'Intent' to commit a crime had to be more strictly proved and negligence had to be determined by a subjective standard instead of an objective one as before. This meant that the test was what it was reasonable for the defendant to have foreseen and not what he should have foreseen. The doctrine of analogy came under attack by jurists on the grounds that it could be used to violate the law and placed the judges above the law, thus undermining its stability. As a consequence the draft criminal code of 1940 omitted any reference to analogy but the draft was dropped with the onset of the Second World War and analogy remained until after the death of Stalin.[31]

---

30. Getty and Naumov. *Op. cit.,* pp.548-9.
31. See Peter H. Solomon, Jr. *Soviet Criminologists and Criminal Policy: Specialists in Policy-Making.* (London, The Macmillan Press Ltd., 1978), pp.26-7.

Confessions and Torture

In the Soviet Union law had to be an effective and legitimizing instrument of the government and, above all, the Party. Against those who thought otherwise, particularly the Old Bolsheviks, the chief weapons were laws such as article 58 and Stalin's special boards of the NKVD – precisely the laws and agencies that Lenin had said should wither away soon after the Revolution. Indeed, in 1940 in his book *The Soviet Judicial System*, Vyshinsky gave explicit approval to the administrative measure of the NKVD whose special boards condemned people *in absentia*, secretly and without right of defence or appeal. Nonetheless, they were illegal bodies, outside the Constitution, to which the principles of legality meant nothing.

And, in 1941, in his *Theory of Judicial Evidence,* Vyshinsky openly admitted that the confessions of an accused (extracted under torture) were of decisive importance in the trials of the terror. He preferred, he said, a half confession by the accused in his own handwriting to a full confession recorded by the interrogator to make it appear more voluntary.[32] However, protests of victims against unlawful methods used against them were not to be recorded. Furthermore, the probability of guilt was adequate for sentence and this could be detected by political flair rather than evidence.

It is interesting that in his earlier disputes with

---

32. *Cf. Sovietskoye Gosudarstvoi I Pravo.* No.3. March 1965.

Krylenko, Vyshinsky, a moderate jurist in the mid-1930s, had attacked the idea that a confession was sufficient evidence in itself. 'Nothing could be more mistaken,' he said, 'than such a point of view, which has nothing in common with a correct understanding of the tasks of the soviet investigation, of soviet procedure.' It reflected 'procedural backwardness, which is reactionary, harmful, and dangerous for investigation based on the principles of proletarian democracy. It is not by chance that the martial law statute of Peter the Great built its system of evidence on the personal confession of the accused.'[33] By 1940 however Stalin had perceived the virtues of the Tsar and Vyshinsky, of course, stoutly followed his leader.

The methods used during months of interrogation to obtain confessions by Soviet interrogators included confinement in a punishment cell too small to move in, intolerable pressure by teams of inquisitors working for hours and days at a stretch, savage beatings, prolonged deprivation of sleep, and promises of leniency or pardon in return for co-operation. On occasion a person unknown to the accused would be brought face to face with him and shot if the accused remained stubborn. After two or three such brutal murders the accused usually capitulated. Physical torture was normally reserved for those who were not destined to face public trial. And, as already seen with Old Bolsheviks, loved ones, including young children, were frequently held hostage and threatened with death unless

---

33. Quoted by Eugene Huskey. *Vyshinskii, Krylenko, and the Shaping of the Soviet Legal Order. (Slavic Review, Op. cit,* 1987), pp.421-2.

the prisoner confessed. Not for the Soviet regime were political prisoners to be allowed to turn the tables on their accusers as often happened in Tsarist times.

Khrushchev, in his secret speech, spoke of the appalling torture of Politburo candidate member Lev Eikhe, a Party member since 1905, who had arrested many 'Trotskyites' who ironically then gave false evidence against him. Eikhe wrote to Stalin explaining how his 'confession' had been fabricated by his interrogators but Stalin merely passed the letter to Beria and Eikhe was shot in 1940. Subsequent investigations confirmed that the case against him was false and he was posthumously rehabilitated. Khrushchev also revealed that another Old Bolshevik, Kedrov, wrote to the Central Committee concerning Beria's treacherous activities. In response, Kedrov was arraigned and tried but was found by the Military Collegium to be innocent of the charges brought against him. This failed to save him however, and he was subsequently shot on Beria's orders.[34]

A.T. Cholerton, long resident in Moscow as a British newspaper correspondent, when asked whether *habeas corpus* operated in the USSR replied that, 'whatever might be the case with *habeas corpus*, the authorities strictly adhered to *habeas cadavar*.'[35]

As for the cruel physical tortures in the concentration camps, they are graphically described by Solzhenitzyn in

---

34. Khrushchev. *Secret Speech. Op. cit.*
35. Malcolm Muggeridge. *Chronicles of Wasted Time.* (Glasgow, Fontana/Collins, 1975), vol.i, p.271.

One Day in the Life of Ivan Denisovich[36] and *The Gulag Archipelago*[37] and in Eugenia Ginzburg's *Into the Whirlwind.*[38] The latter wrote from personal experience of the interrogators that 'They were all sadists of course. And only a handful found the courage to commit suicide. Pace by pace, as they followed one routine directive after another they climbed down the steps from the human condition to that of beasts.'[39] Many prisoners were indeed worked to death in the camps under atrocious conditions. But prior to her arrest, and despite the fact that people she had known and trusted were disappearing, Ginzburg knew she herself was innocent and showed a lack of comprehension of what was going on, as did the bulk of the population who felt also that there could be no smoke without fire. And the peasant population, including those who had gone to the towns and were working in industry, brought up on tales of witchcraft and evil spirits could be persuaded to believe in 'enemies of the people'.

In May 1947 the death penalty was abolished for all crimes and in the following month capital punishment for stealing socialist property was replaced by 7 to 10 years' deprivation of freedom in a labour camp,[40] although this could be doubled without a hearing by administrative decree. On the other hand, in the same year the minimum sentence of three months' imprisonment for theft of

---

36. (London, Victor Gollancz Ltd., 1970).
37. *Op. cit.*
38. (London, Penguin Books, 1968).
39. *Ibid.,* p.54.
40. *Gazette of the Supreme Soviet.* (1947), number 19 (473).

personal property was increased to five years and for rape the penalty of from one to five years was increased to from 10 to 15 years.[41]

At the same time, so far as theft is concerned Stalin had enacted new laws which provided for harsh sentences for all categories of theft in place of a differentiated set of punishments. For instance, petty theft which had formerly been punished with a sentence of three months corrective work was now subject to a minimum sentence of five years in a camp. The punishment for theft of state property was set at 7 to 10 years imprisonment and for a second offence, or as a member of an organized group (which was not defined), the sentence was 10 to 25 years in the camps, even for 14-year-olds. These laws against thieves, whom Stalin saw as traitors, were his most repressive measures against ordinary criminals, as distinct from political prisoners.[42] And on 12 January 1950 the death penalty was restored for traitors, spies, subversives and saboteurs,[43] which could include theft of state-owned property.

The War

During the 'Great Patriotic War' from 1941 to 1945 Stalin had other things on his mind but the purges continued and

---

41. *Ibid.* and *RSFSR Criminal Code*, 1957, p.127.
42. Peter H. Solomon, Jr. *Op. cit.,* pp.27-8.
43. *Gazette of the Supreme Soviet.* Number 3 (618).

indeed just prior to the German invasion in June 1941, 134,000 people from the Baltic States, which the Soviet Union had absorbed by agreement with Hitler, were sent to camps run by the NKVD. Then, towards the close of the war when the Red Army was advancing westwards whole peoples, including the Chechens, Crimean Tartars, Steppe Kalmyks and others were deported to Siberia *en masse*. Out of one and a half million of such people some half a million are believed to have died in appalling conditions *en route* to the Gulag. When the war ended, although the Soviet Union was victorious Russian soldiers who had been taken prisoner by the Germans and survived (and millions died in captivity) were treated as enemies and sent to the camps.[44] Further purges took place during post-war re-collectivization in areas the German army had occupied when more people were deported from the Baltic States and the Ukraine as well as the Cossacks.

The Leningrad Affair

After the war, during which over 20 million soldiers and civilians had died, the 1930s purges within the Party seemed set to be re-enacted with Stalin's top aides and likely successors, such as Zhdanov, Beria and Malenkov, feeding his paranoia with allegations against each others supporters. Although Stalin's prestige was high the people were hopeful of change after all their tremendous efforts

---

44. *Gazette of the Supreme Soviet*, number 3 (618).

and suffering in the war. Instead, Stalin decided on further repression and the cutting off of Russia from all outside influences. Zhdanov, who in the inter-Party disputes was a moderate (although moderation was a relative term), launched a series of hard-line attacks on decadent art and the scientific, literary and academic world was subjected to severe persecution.

Then suddenly, in 1948, Zhdanov, who was the Party boss in Leningrad and Stalin's heir apparent, died after being demoted at the instigation of his rivals in the leadership, and the years 1949/50 saw the arrest on Stalin's orders of a number of leaders of the Party organization in the city. Among them were Zhdanov's protégés, Nikolai Voznesensky, a celebrated economist, member of the Politburo, deputy chairman of the Council of Ministers and chairman of Gosplan, Alexis Kuznetsov, a secretary of the Central Committee and a leader of the defence of Leningrad and other Ministers. These were not Old Bolsheviks but beneficiaries of upward mobility that occurred during Stalin's purges who had served him loyally but fell victim to the leadership power struggles that existed during Stalin's declining years.

In 1948 Voznesensky had published a book dealing with the economy during the war. It enjoyed great success and was awarded the Stalin Prize. Stalin had read the book in manuscript, authorized its publication and approved it for the prize. Yet suddenly he found it to be anti-Marxist and it was withdrawn from circulation whilst Voznesensky was removed from all his posts. Perhaps Stalin had decided that the book showed too clearly the economic strength of the United States in comparison with the Soviet Union or one of his aides had planted seeds of suspicion against Voznesensky in his susceptible mind.

In any event, Stalin, who a few years later was to publish his *Economic Problems of Socialism in the USSR* and be acclaimed as the greatest of scientists, considered himself to be an economic genius. And that was dangerous since as Bukharin, who knew Stalin intimately, had told Trotsky, the dictator had 'an implacable jealousy of anyone who knows more or does things better than he.'[45] Brought to trial on charges of losing papers in Gosplan, Voznesensky declared his innocence and in the absence of any evidence against him he was released. Not for long however. In spite of his closeness to Stalin and the continued absence of any evidence of wrongdoing, in 1950 he was re-arrested, charged with treason and shot. According to Khrushchev's secret speech the evidence at the trial was fabricated by Beria and his deputy on Stalin's instructions.[46]

Altogether, some 2,000 Party cadres, many of them Zhdanov's supporters were purged, and executed or deported to labour camps by Stalin in what became known as 'the Leningrad Affair', at the prompting, according to Khrushchev, of Zhdanov's rivals Malenkov and Beria who took his place at Stalin's right hand. The 'Affair' was not made public at the time and was revealed only after

---

45. Robert Conquest. *The Nation Killers: The Soviet Deportation of Nationalities.* (London, Macmillan, 1970.)
46. Secret Speech. *Op. cit.,* p.598.

Stalin's death.

A little later came the Mingrelian Affair, directed at Beria, himself a Mingrelian, and his followers who were purged. According to Khrushchev's secret speech, on the basis of forged documents loyal communists in Georgia were alleged to have formed a nationalist organization with the aim of destroying Soviet power in that republic with the help of imperialist powers. The allegations, he said, were nonsense but they resulted in the deaths of thousands of innocent people through lawlessness.

The 'Doctors' Plot'

On 13 January 1953 *Pravda* announced that an organization of nine physicians, seven of them Jewish, had been unmasked and the criminals arrested. The investigation was carried out under Stalin's personal direction by S.D. Ignatyev, the new secret police chief. It was alleged that they had murdered a number of Soviet leaders, including Andrei Zhdanov in August 1948, shortened the life of A.S. Shcherbakov, head of the Moscow Party organization, and attempted to kill a number of marshals and admirals. With echoes of the past they were accused of being American spies but to this it was added that they were also in the pay of an international Jewish organization. In consequence of this last allegation thousands of Jewish specialists were expelled from hospitals, laboratories and medical schools in a wave of anti-semitism in which Jews were branded as 'zionists' and 'rootless cosmopolitans'.

The security services were accused by Stalin of a 'lack of vigilance' which suggested that another purge was unfolding in which Lavrenti Beria, now head of the MGB (Ministry of State Security) – the reorganized NKVD – might become a victim. Indeed, Khrushchev believed that Stalin was about to destroy the old members of the Politburo and that Voroshilov, Molotov and Mikoyan were under suspicion.[47] Stalin accused Voroshilov of being an English agent and Molotov's wife was exiled. At the Nineteenth Party Congress it was decided to create a Praesidium of 25 members as a cover, according to Krushschev, 'for the future annihilation of the old Politburo members.'[48] However, no trial or blood-bath took place as Stalin died suddenly two months later, on 5 March, and the case was dropped.

Legality

The concept of legality in democratic countries comprises a system of law, guarantees for its implementation and minimum legal standards. The last, now enshrined in the Universal Declaration of Human Rights of 1948, include the presumption of innocence, the inviolability of the person, the independence of judges, the equality of all

---

47. Merve Fainsod. *How Russia is Ruled.* (Cambridge, Mass. Harvard University Press, 1963), p.447.
48. Secret Speech. *Op. cit.,* p.615.

citizens before the law and the courts, and open and fair court hearings.[49] As we have seen, not one of these operated in criminal law in Stalin's Russia.

In contrast, in 1940 two Soviet jurists, S.A. Golunsky and M.S. Strogovich published *The Theory of the State and Law*[50] in which they continued the theme that 'law dictates the will of the dominant class to the subordinate classes in order to hold them obedient.'[51] They also gave the official interpretation of the relationship between socialist law and socialist legality. 'Socialist law,' they wrote, 'is indissolubly connected with socialist legality. Socialist legality is the method of making the proletarian dictatorship and the building up of socialism effective; it is expressed in guaranteeing that all organs of the Soviet state, official personages, and citizens strictly and unswervingly observe the legislation enacted by Soviet authority.'[52] How many millions suffered from it not being so, from the myth diverging from reality, will never be accurately known.

---

49. See Ivo Lapenna. *Lenin, Law and Legality.* In Leonard Shapiro and Peter Reddaway, eds. *Lenin, the Man, the Theorist, the Leader: A Reappraisal.* (London, Pall Mall Press, 1967), p.239.
50. The Institute of Law of the USSR. (Moscow, 1940), in Hugh W. Babb. *Soviet Legal Philosophy. Op. cit.*
51. *Ibid.,* p.337.
52. *Ibid.,* p.392.

CHAPTER 9

Afterword

Most of the books published dealing with Stalin's Russia portray a story of horror. This one is no exception. Yet Stalin, like Lenin, considered himself to be an enlightened leader. But both were born into the culture and background of long-standing Tsarist autocracy with its centralized and unrestricted power and no tradition of representative institutions, liberty or the rule of law. Marx and Engels, in contrast, were aligned with the European Romantic movement which drew its inspiration from the Renaissance. They accepted the historical role of industrial capitalism but abhorred its 'dark satanic mills' and offered a vision of a humanistic (perhaps utopian) society of the future for mankind.

Seizing power, and drunk with power, in a backward peasant empire Lenin and Stalin destroyed that visionary element in their own adopted ideology. Violence, coupled with a cynical disregard for human beings and a belief that the end justifies the means, were an integral part of their creed. Marx spent most of his life analysing capitalism and believed that by historical necessity force would have to be used to change society. But, as we have seen, after surveying the Paris Commune and approving its violence, he wrote in his *The Civil War in France* that the proletarian state should be based on universal suffrage with representatives subject to recall and exercising both executive and legislative powers.[1] In time that state would wither away and become obsolete in a more humane society.

Lenin, on the contrary, taking from Marx what suited him and ignoring what did not, arbitrarily destroyed the Constituent Assembly which had been elected countrywide and took the idea of holding on to power by unrestrained violence as his benchmark. He believed absolutely in the social regimentation of mankind. In an empire with a small proletariat, a vast and downtrodden peasantry and large national minorities this was a recipe for long-term disaster. All that can be said in his favour is that he believed that the proletariat in the advanced industrial countries would also seize power and come to his assistance. But when that prospect receded he remained undaunted about the exercise of state terror against the bulk of the population. The vision of the future was dispelled by the very means used to attempt to attain it.

One question that arises is, was Lenin's the correct and only path to take once the Revolution had succeeded? Mikhail Gorbachev once argued that it was and that Stalin diverted from it. The evidence that Lenin prepared the ground for Stalin which is set out in the early part of this book overwhelmingly shows otherwise. A more important question is whether the Soviet system might have succeeded if its leaders had not been tyrants. In fact, all

---

1. *Op. cit.*, p.471.

the early measures of terror were undertaken not only by Lenin and Stalin but by Trotsky, Bukharin, Zinoviev and virtually all their comrades. As senior Bolsheviks were picked off by Stalin and executed after being falsely accused of crimes that to them were unimaginable it is possible to feel a certain sympathy for the way they had been framed and 'tried'. But that is to forget that while in power they, too, participated in the tyranny and probably deserved their fate. Only if they had been prepared to share power and proceed by other means might events have taken a different turn and that is speculation and cannot be assessed. As is well known, the 'ifs' of history, however entertaining, are never open to solution.

Lenin's utter determination, at whatever cost, not to relinquish power once it had been won meant that he turned many supporters into enemies and, in his eyes, necessitated the use of unlimited terror. And this can be seen as a logical progression from the lessons that he drew from the Paris Commune. Although by 1917 Russia was ripe for the revolution against Tsarism that erupted in February the Bolsheviks were not ready for power and achieved it only by a coup, as Gorbachev admitted. Unlike that of the Mensheviks from whom they split, the programme of the Bolsheviks did not admit of democracy. As a consequence, the principle of centralism at the heart of their determinedly small Party of professional revolutionaries was inculcated into government and social life with the result that the dictatorship of the proletariat became first the dictatorship of the Party and then of the leader, as Rosa Luxemburg, Karl Kautsky and other

Marxists warned it would.

Was then the philosophy and practice of Lenin, combined with the backwardness of Russia, where it went wrong or could the collapse into terror have been avoided if a state had been established based on Marxist principles? Alternatively, were those principles flawed from the beginning? Marx made a penetrating analysis of the capitalist system but he could not foresee the road to the future he predicted. Indeed, he could not even see clearly the future of capitalist society. With his internationalist vision he grossly underestimated the growing strength of nationalism throughout the world. His forecast of the growing impoverishment of the working class in industrial societies did not materialize, nor did he foresee the diminution in size of that class. Furthermore, with Engels, he always maintained that force was the midwife of the new society. So far at least, violent overthrow of the state has not proved to be the way forward to a better life that the majority of the working class, or any other class, have wished to adopt. Although Lenin adapted Marxist theory in Russian conditions he remained a Marxist in essentials and it is difficult to see how followers of Marx could have taken a democratic path. This has subsequently also been shown in China, a number of African countries and elsewhere when Marxist dictatorships have been established. After all, it was Marx himself who conceived the concept of the 'dictatorship of the proletariat'.

The Whig, and Marxist, view of historical progress is no longer widely accepted. The terrible twentieth century, as

Winston Churchill called it, with genocide, Hitler, the Holocaust, Stalinism and the threat of nuclear warfare has seen to that. At the beginning of the twenty-first century modern society, with all its wealth and technology, is now not only far removed from early capitalism yet in some respects remains powered by corporate greed and selfishness, with obscene differences between rich and poor. Surveying today's world with its divisions between advanced and undeveloped countries, with its wars and endemic violence, with dire prospects from nuclear proliferation and monopoly globalization, the question that remains for many people is whether a humanistic vision for the future of all mankind can be revived and be brought to fruition. It is to be hoped so, but the journey promises to be a long one and Stalin's Russia continues to signal a warning against taking the wrong path. Revolutionary law, which is really no law at all, is no substitute for the rule of law.

Appendix

Brief Biographies of Key Figures of the Period

Beria, Lavrenti

Beria's early years are obscure but it is known that he was born in Georgia on 29 March 1899 and joined the Party in 1917. His early Revolutionary career was confined to Azerbaijan and Georgia, first in the Cheka and then in the Party machine. He became a member of the Central Committee in 1934 but it was not until July 1938 that he was called to Moscow by Stalin to replace Yezhov and become overlord of the security services and the Gulag. In this role he became Stalin's bloody right hand and apart from the purges he is widely believed to have been responsible for the massacre of thousands of Polish officers and intellectuals at the Katyn forest near Smolensk. During the war he was made a member of the State Defence Committee and after the war, when a member of the Politburo, he was in charge of the development of the Soviet atomic bomb. After Stalin's death the dictator's successors, against whom Beria had flaunted his powers, made him a scapegoat for their own crimes and had him shot in December 1953 as an 'imperialist agent'.

Bukharin, Nikolai

Bukharin was born in Moscow on 27 September 1888. Both his parents were middle-class school teachers. As a student he became interested in Marxist literature and in 1906 he joined the Bolshevik wing of the Russian Social Democratic Workers' Party. After spells of imprisonment for Revolutionary activities, prior to the Revolution in February 1917 he spent six years in exile in Western Europe, where he met Lenin and Stalin, and in the United States, where he met Trotsky. In America he edited a Bolshevik newspaper, *Novy Mir* (The New World), and for a short time Trotsky assisted him despite their differences on political issues. On returning to Russia in 1917 he played an important part in the Bolshevik Revolution in Moscow and strongly supported the policies of War Communism. He became a member of the Central Committee of the Party and as a leader of the Left Communists he opposed the Brest-Litovsk peace treaty with Germany. In 1920 he published *The Politics and Economics of the Transitional Period* and in 1921 the famous *ABC of Communism* (with Yevgeny Preobrazhensky) and *The Theory of Historical Materialism*, each of which enhanced his position in the leadership of the Party.

He was a member of the Central Committee and the Politburo from 1919 to 1929 when he was removed by Stalin as a 'right-oppositionist' despite their former close political association. He was editor of *Pravda* from 1918 to 1929 and of *Izvestia*, the official government newspaper, from 1934 to 1937. A member of the Communist International from 1919 to 1929, he was its chairman for three years before Stalin had him removed. In 1934 he gravely warned the Party of the danger of Hitler while Stalin was brushing it aside. He wrote many Marxist theoretical works and was responsible for much of the Constitution of 1936. In 1937-8 he was arrested, tried and shot in the Great Terror for alleged counter-Revolutionary activity and espionage. He was posthumously re-instated as a Party member in 1988.

Kamenev, Lev

Kamenev was born to middle-class parents (themselves Revolutionaries) in Moscow on 18 July 1883 and moved with his family to Tiflis in 1896. He studied law at Moscow University but was arrested in 1902 and, after a spell in jail, went abroad. In Paris he joined the Bolsheviks in 1903 and soon married Trotsky's sister, Olga. After the 1903 Party Congress Lenin sent him back to Russia where he was active mostly in Tiflis and the Caucasus. In 1914 he was in St. Petersburg editing *Pravda* but was soon arrested and sent to Siberia where at the time of the February Revolution he was in exile with Stalin. On their return to St. Petersburg, now re-named Petrograd, they both assumed leadership of the Party and gave conditional support to Kerensky's Provisional Government. However, when Lenin returned to Russia in April 1917 he insisted that the Bolsheviks should oppose the government and attempt to seize power at the first favourable opportunity. Stalin accepted this strategy but Kamenev joined Zinoviev in opposing the Bolshevik seizure of power in October and leaked the date of the coup. They also opposed a Party decision not to seek a coalition with the Mensheviks and other parties. Lenin was furious but soon brought them both back into the leadership with Kamenev a member of Lenin's first Politburo, and chairman of the Central Executive Committee of the All-Russian Congress of Soviets.

When Lenin became seriously ill in 1922 Kamenev and Zinoviev joined Stalin in opposing Trotsky but when subsequently attacked and defeated by Stalin they turned to Trotsky to form the 'United Opposition'. Although of a mild and conciliatory temperament, Kamenev openly opposed Stalin at the Fourteenth Party Congress in 1925 and from then on his fate was sealed. Accused with Zinoviev of being morally responsible for the assassination of Kirov he was first imprisoned and after his second trial in 1935, in which he was found guilty of treason, he was shot. In 1988 he was posthumously cleared of all charges by the Soviet Supreme Court.

Kirov, Sergei

Kirov joined the Party at the age of 18 in Tomsk in 1904. He was active in organizing the Transcaucasian Soviet Republic in 1922 which at the end of that year was incorporated into the USSR. Stalin transferred him in 1926 to head the Party in Leningrad and he was elected to the Politburo in 1930. An effective orator, in 1934 as head of the Leningrad Party machine for the past 10 years and showing some independence he was in a powerful position and was seen by many as Stalin's successor. At the Party Congress in January/February that year he is said to have secured more votes for election to the Central Committee than Stalin. On 1 December of the same year, at the age of 48, he was shot in the back of the head in the Smolny Institute by Leonid Nikolayev. A widespread purge of Leningrad citizens followed on Stalin's orders. Khrushchev, in his secret speech on 25 February 1956, strongly suggested that Stalin was responsible for the assassination.

Lenin, Vladimir Ilyich

Lenin was born Ulyanov into a middle-class family in Simbirsk (later re-named Ulyanov after him) in the Russian Federation in 1870. His father was a civil servant who served long enough to attain the equivalent rank of general and hereditary membership of the nobility.[1] Lenin was deeply affected by the execution of his elder brother Alexander for conspiracy to kill the Tsar and had a strong belief in violence as part of the evolution of society, but not assassination which he considered futile. He was educated in law at Kazan University, where he proved to be intellectually gifted, and in 1892 began to practise law.

Soon engaging in illegal revolutionary activity he was exiled to Siberia for three years. He then moved to Switzerland and began to edit the newspaper *Iskra* (The Spark). In his book *What is to be Done*, published in 1902, he advocated a Party of professional activists to spearhead the Revolution which after success in October 1917 was to form the basis of Communist Parties throughout the world. At the 1903 Congress of the Russian Social Democratic Workers' Party, held in Brussels and London he split the Party by forming its Bolshevik wing based on that concept of a vanguard Party in opposition to the more moderate Mensheviks. The split was made permanent in 1912 when he turned the Bolsheviks into their own Party. He wrote profusely on Marxism, often in violent polemic with other Marxists such as Kautsky, Plekhanov and Rosa Luxemburg who correctly foresaw the dictatorship of the proletariat turning into the dictatorship of a centralist and undemocratic Party.

After the February Revolution in Russia in 1917 Lenin returned to Petrograd in a German sealed train and presented to the Party his *April Theses* calling for a Revolution based on Soviets of workers, soldiers and peasants. Calling for 'All Power to the Soviets' Lenin persuaded the Central Committee of the Party to agree to aim for an armed insurrection to destroy the Provisional Government which had been formed after February. In October the government was overthrown and Lenin was

---

1. Nicolas Berdyaev. *The Origin of Russian Communism.* (London, Geoffrey Bles: The Centenary Press, 1937), p.138.

elected by the Soviets as chairman of the Council of People's Commissars. Following the October Revolution he had the elected Constituent Assembly, in which the Bolsheviks were in a minority, dissolved and proclaimed the dictatorship of the proletariat. Civil war, in which he advocated terror, and a collapse of the economy followed and caused him to introduce the New Economic Policy – a form of mixed economy. He was shot and injured in 1918 and died on 21 January 1924. His body was embalmed in a crystal casket in a mausoleum in Red Square in Moscow. In his testament he proposed the removal of Stalin from the post of General-Secretary of the Party but despite his wish this was not read to the Thirteenth Party Congress and Stalin remained in the post and his ascendancy over the Party became assured. Accepted as the architect of the Revolution, Lenin's prestige was such that during his lifetime his leadership was never challenged, although some of his policies were. However, he was directly responsible for the dictatorship of the Party, the terror and totalitarian rule.

Pashukanis, Evgeny

A Russian legal philosopher, Pashukanis was born on 10 February 1891 in the city of Staritsa. A graduate of St Petersburg University's law faculty he was a student of Pavel Stuchka. Little known until the early 1920s, he was the author of *A General Theory of Law and Marxism* published in 1924 in which he contended that law was a feature of societies which practised commodity exchange through markets. He strongly believed that law was essentially bourgeois in character and could not be given a socialist content. In any event, as part of the state machine it would 'wither away' under socialism as forecast by Engels. Hence, as law would have little future in socialist society he downgraded the teaching of law and thought the civil and criminal codes would be temporary in the Soviet Union. This view was popular in the 1920s but began to lose favour when Stalin decided that strong laws were needed to secure discipline in a society undergoing violent change. Pashukanis accordingly admitted to some mistakes and was appointed Vice-Commissar of Justice in 1936. However, he was finally overtaken by Vyshinsky in the Great Terror and was arrested and shot. Nevertheless, his work has been more influential outside Russia than that of any other Marxist legal philosopher.

Rykov, Alexei

Rykov was born in 1881 and joined the Party in 1899. He was appointed a member of the Central Committee in 1906 becoming People's Commissar for the Interior in the first Soviet government in 1917. A member of the Politburo, on Lenin's death he succeeded him as Chairman of the Council of People's Commissars of the USSR (Premier) and was a member of the Praesidium of the powerful Central Executive Committee. A strong supporter of NEP he joined with Bukharin and Tomsky in the leadership of the so-called 'Right Opposition' in 1928. With Stalin's ascendancy he was removed from all his posts and expelled from the Party in 1929. He was re-admitted in 1931 and became People's Commissar of Communications from 1931 to 1936. He was expelled from the Party again in 1937 and in the following year shared the trial and fate of Bukharin.

Stalin, Joseph

Stalin was born Josif Dzhugashvili to a peasant couple in the small Georgian town of Gori on 9 December 1879. His early life was spent in poverty in a harsh environment. By his mother's wish he was educated first in the Gori church school and later at the seminary in Tiflis where he rebelled against the strict and oppressive discipline. From there he graduated to revolutionary.

He joined the Bolshevik Party in 1898, and was involved in revolutionary work in Transcaucasia. He was active in the October Revolution and subsequently carried out a number of military tasks for Lenin during the civil war and in 1925 had the city of Tsaritsyn renamed Stalingrad after his exploits there. Following the October Revolution he was made People's Commissar of Nationalities. In April 1922 he became General-Secretary of the Party and avoided attempts by Lenin and others to have him removed from the post. At various stages he secured the expulsion from the Party of Trotsky, who was to call him 'the outstanding mediocrity of our Party', and his one-time allies, but potential rivals, Zinoviev, Kamenev and Bukharin. He espoused the concept of 'socialism in one country' and after proclaiming the intensification of the class struggle he commenced purge trials and introduced rapid industrialization and collectivization. His campaign to eliminate the kulaks as a class had a disastrous effect upon agriculture, with something like 10 million peasants perishing, and brought about a terrible famine. However, he was responsible for the building of a heavy industrial complex which bore fruit in the defeat of the Nazi war machine in the Second World War.

After the assassination of Kirov in 1934 (which he may have engineered) he instigated the Great Terror in which countless millions of people went to their deaths. Nineteen-thirty-nine saw the Hitler-Stalin Pact which divided Poland between Germany and Russia with the latter also incorporating the Baltic states. During the war he assumed the post of Supreme Commander of the Armed Forces and after a bad start led the Red Army to victory. In 1949 he commenced a new series of Party purges but died in dubious circumstances on 5 March 1953 before the accused in the 'Doctors' Plot' could be brought to trial.

Stuchka, Pavel Ivanovich

Born in Riga on 14 August 1865 of a peasant family, Stuchka, like Pashukanis who became his pupil, was also a graduate of St Petersburg University's law faculty and he became an active revolutionary in his early twenties. From 1888 he was editor of Latvian social democratic newspapers until 1897 when he was exiled to the upper reaches of the Volga. After the 1905 Revolution he returned from exile to St. Petersburg, became an active Bolshevik and defended many revolutionaries in the Tsarist courts in the city. During the February Revolution of 1917 he became a member of the Petrograd Soviet. In March 1918 he became Commissar of Justice in the Bolshevik government in succession to Dr Isaac Steinberg, a member of the Left Socialist Revolutionary Party. In 1920-21 he was a member of the Central Committee of the Party and was highly regarded as a jurist who saw the need for proletarian law until the law withered away. In the meantime he was appointed chairman of the Supreme Court of the Russian Federation in 1923. He represented Latvia in the Comintern and was for many years an official in the secret police. He died peacefully on 25 January 1932 at the age of 67.

Trotsky, Lev Davidovich

Born Bronstein in the village of Yanovka in the Ukraine of a Jewish small farmer in 1879 Trotsky was converted to Marxism in 1897 after attending the University of Odessa. After having worked with Lenin, at the Second Social Democratic Party Congress, held in Brussels and London in July 1903, he joined the Mensheviks and made a vitriolic attack on Lenin whom he denounced as a 'Robespierre' who desired to establish a 'dictatorship over the proletariat'. He was president of the St.

Petersburg Soviet in the 1905 Revolution and two years later was exiled to Siberia for the second time. After his escape he spent some time during the war years in Western Europe engaging in anti-war agitation and finally reached New York in January 1917 where he joined Bukharin in editing the Russian-language newspaper *Novy Mir* (The New World). Although Bukharin was a Bolshevik, Trotsky, formerly a Menshevik, did not join the Bolsheviks until August 1917 when he was immediately elected to the Central Committee of the Party. After returning to Russia, he led the Petrograd Soviet again in the 1917 Bolshevik coup and in the civil war he was leader of the Red Army which led to his great authority and prestige. As Commissar for War he built the new Red Army as a disciplined and professional force using former Tsarist officers under the supervision of Communist commissars.

In the name of permanent revolution he fought against the idea of socialism in one country declaring that the Revolution was bound to lead to serious conflicts between the proletariat and the peasantry which could only be resolved by a world-wide proletarian revolution. This approach and his arrogance tended to isolate him, however, and on Lenin's death his rivals joined forces to block his potential claim to be Lenin's political heir and he was subsequently denigrated until his expulsion from the Party and the Soviet Union by Stalin. In exile abroad he kept in touch with his supporters inside the Soviet Union but, constantly under attack in the purge trials, his influence declined and he was finally killed in Mexico on Stalin's orders in 1940.

Vyshinsky, Andrei

Vyshinsky was born in Odessa on 28 November 1883 of Polish descent. He studied law at Kiev University from which he was expelled for illegal Marxist activity. He joined the Menshevik wing when Lenin split the Russian Social Democratic Workers' Party and formed the Bolshevik wing. In February 1920 he became a Bolshevik and served as prosecutor of the RSFSR from 1923-25. He was appointed rector of Moscow State University in the latter year and three years later presided over the Shakhty trial and the trial of the Industrial Party in 1930. A staunch supporter of Stalin, as deputy prosecutor from 1933, and procurator-general from 1935, he prosecuted in all the major state trials of the 1930s. With the denunciation of Pashukanis he became head of the Institute of Law of the Academy of Sciences and spokesman for the new jurisprudence. In 1940 he supervised the incorporation of Latvia into the Soviet Union and at the end of the war, in 1945, he was instrumental in securing communist power in Rumania. In March 1949 he became foreign minister and ambassador to the United Nations. He committed suicide on board ship when recalled from New York to Moscow after the death of Stalin, doubtless aware of the fate that was in store for him.

Yagoda, Genrikh

Yagoda was born in 1891 and joined the Bolshevik Party in 1907. He filled various posts immediately after the Revolution but his future in the Party was determined when he was appointed to the Praesidium of the Cheka in 1920. He was deputy Chairman of Cheka's successor organization, the OGPU, from 1924 to 1934 and head of the Gulag in 1930 when he also became a candidate member of the Central Committee. In 1934 he became head of the NKVD and a full member of the Central Committee. He was almost certainly involved, on Stalin's orders, in the assassination of Kirov and was active in the early state trials in which Zinoviev, Kamenev and their associates were executed. But he displeased Stalin by his alleged tardiness in bringing Bukharin

181

to trial and was replaced as head of the NKVD by Yezhov in 1936 for 'crimes in office'. He was arrested in 1937 and he too shared Bukharin's fate, being shot in March 1938. He is said to have privately supported Bukharin and Rykov in 1929/30.

Yezhov, Nicolai

Yezhov was born into a working class family in 1895 in St. Petersburg and he joined the Party only in March 1917. Little is known of his early life. However, he served in the civil war as a front line commander and was Deputy Commissar of Agriculture during the collectivization in 1929-30. He had become one of Stalin's new men when appointed to work in the offices of the Central Committee in 1927. On 29 April 1933 he became a member of the Central Purge Commission which expelled more than a million members from the Party. In 1935 he was elected secretary of the Central Committee and made chairman of the Party's powerful Control Commission. On Stalin's orders, in September 1936 he replaced Yagoda as People's Commissar for Internal Affairs in order to conduct the Great Terror. He denounced Yagoda as a Tsarist police spy and an embezzler and had 3,000 of Yagoda's NKVD officers executed. Some five feet in height and lame he was known as the 'bloodthirsty dwarf' and his reign of terror as head of the NKVD became known as the terrible 'Yezhovshchina' during which many millions of people perished. At the end of 1938 he was accused of being a Polish spy and was arrested and replaced by Beria. He was tried *in camera* in February 1940 and his fate remains unknown, although S. Swianiewicz, who was herself imprisoned in the Lubyanka, in her book *Forced Labour and Economic Development*[2] claims to

2.   *Op. cit.*

have some evidence that he was still alive in prison in 1941 and was well treated.

Zinoviev, Grigori

He was born to lower-class Jewish parents in 1883 in Elizavetgrad (re-named Zinoviesk in 1924). Educated at home he never attended school or university, although whilst travelling abroad in 1902-05 he attended lectures on law at Bern University in Switzerland. He had joined the Social Democratic Workers' Party in 1901 and, after the Party split in 1903 he was a member of Lenin's Bolshevik wing. Although he carried out Party work in St. Petersburg in the 1905 Revolution he was not popular and owed his subsequent position in the leadership of the Party from his close collaboration with Lenin from 1909 to 1917. After the outbreak of the February Revolution in 1917 he returned to Petrograd in April with Lenin in the famous German sealed train. With Kamenev he incurred Lenin's anger when they made public the plans for the October *coup d'état* but was soon forgiven.

By 1921 he was head of the Petrograd Party organization and a member of the Politburo. He became the first president of the Communist International in March 1919. With Kamenev and Stalin he opposed Trotsky's succession to Lenin after the latter's death in January 1924 but was soon outmanoeuvred by Stalin. In January 1935 he was arrested with Kamenev and 17 others and charged with the moral and political responsibility for Kirov's murder and was sentenced to 10 years' imprisonment. Later he was brought to court again, sentenced to death and executed. Like Kamenev he was completely exonerated of all crimes alleged against him during the purge trials by the Soviet Supreme Court in 1988.

Chronology

1917

February	The February Revolution
March	Abdication of the Tsar: formation of the Provisional Government
June	First All-Russian Congress of Soviets assembled in Petrograd
July-Sept.	Lenin's *The State and Revolution* written
October	The Bolshevik Revolution
November	First Decree on the Courts issued
December	Left Socialist Revolutionaries join Bolsheviks in coalition government
	Creation of the Cheka by resolution

1918

January	The Constituent Assembly dissolved
February	Second Decree on the Courts issued
March	Brest-Litovsk Treaty with Germany signed
	Left Socialist Revolutionaries resign from government
	Stuchka appointed Commissar of Justice
May	Outbreak of fighting in civil war
	Left Socialist Revolutionaries' attempted coup
July	Soviet Constitution adopted
September	Red Terror proclaimed by decree
November	Law on the People's Courts issued

1919

December	Basic Principles for the Criminal Law published

1920

August	Tambov peasant rising commenced

1921

February	Red Army invasion of Georgia
March	Kronstadt sailors' revolt
	10th Party congress: NEP adopted

1922

February	Cheka reorganized as GPU
March	Lenin's top secret memorandum on Shuya
April	Stalin appointed general secretary of the Party
May	First criminal code of the Russian Federation enacted
	Office of Public Procurator established
	Famine
December	USSR formed

1923

July	USSR constitution published
November	Decree replaces GPU with OGPU

1924

January	Death of Lenin
	Supreme Court set up

1925

April	14th Party congress: 'socialism in one country' adopted

1926

	Russian Criminal Code enacted

1927

June	Article 58 incorporated into the Criminal Code
December	15th Party congress: collectivization of agriculture agreed upon

1928
Spring   Grain procurement crisis
May   The Shakhty trial
October   First Five-Year-Plan

1929
Autumn   Stalin's policy of 'elimination of kulaks as a class' adopted
November   Defeat of 'Right Opposition': Bukharin expelled from Politburo

1930
March   Stalin's 'Dizzy with Success'
November   Trial of 'Industrial Party'

1933
April   Metro-Vickers trial

1934
July   OGPU reorganized as NKVD
December   Kirov assassinated in Leningrad

1935
January   Death of Kuibyshev
            Vyshinsky appointed Procurator-General

1936
August   Trial of Zinoviev and Kamenev
September   Yezhov appointed head of NKVD
December   'Stalin Constitution' adopted

1937
January   Trial of Radek, Pyatakov and others
February   Death of Ordzhonikidze
June   Execution of Tukhachevsky and others
Autumn   Death of Pashukanis in prison

1938

	History of CPSU (B) published
March	Trial of Bukharin, Rykov, Yagoda and others
December	Beria appointed head of NKVD

1948

August	Death of Zhdanov
Autumn	The Leningrad Affair
November	Dissolution of the Jewish Anti-Fascist Committee

1953

| January | The 'Doctors' Plot' |
| March | Death of Stalin |

1956

| February | 20th Party congress: Khrushchev's 'secret speech' |

Bibliography

1. Primary Sources

1917-26. *Decrees: Sob. Uzak.* – Collections of Laws and Regulations of the Worker and Peasant Government. (After 1925 RFSFR added.)

1918. *The First Soviet Constitution.* London. The Labour Publishing Company Ltd.

1922. Bukharin, N. & Preobrazhensky, E. *The ABC of Communism: A Popular Explanation of the Programme of the Communist Party of Russia.* London, The Communist Party of Great Britain.

1930. Stalin, J.V. *Political Report to the Sixteenth Party Congress.* London, Modern Books Ltd.

1930. Trotsky, Leon. *My Life.* London, Butterworth.

1933. *Verbatim Report of the Metro-Vickers Trial heard before the Supreme Court of the USSR.* London. George Allen & Unwin Ltd.

1933. Vyshinsky, Andrei. *Revolutionary Legality on the Present Stage.* Moscow, State Publishing House.

1934. Lenin, Vladimir. *Collected Works,* vol. 26. Moscow, State Publishing House.

1936. *Constitution (Fundamental Law) of the Union of Soviet Socialist Republics.* Moscow, Foreign Languages Publishing House.

1937. *S.Z. Collections of Laws and Regulations of the USSR.*

1937. *Verbatim Report of Court Proceedings in the Case of the Anti-Soviet Trotskyite Centre heard before the Military Collegium of the Supreme Court of the USSR,* Moscow, People's Commissariat of Justice of the USSR.

1937. Lenin, Vladimir. *Selected Works,* vol.7. *State & Revolution.* London, Lawrence & Wishart Ltd.

1938. *Verbatim Report of Court Proceedings of the Anti-Soviet 'Bloc of Rights and Trotskyites' heard before the Military Collegium of the Supreme Court of the USSR.* Moscow, People's Commissariat of Justice of the USSR.

1938. Vyshinsky, Andrei. *The Law of the Soviet State.* New York, The Macmillan Company.

1939. Lenin, Vladimir. *Selected Works,* vol.11, 1939. *The Theoretical Principles of Marxism.* London, Lawrence & Wishart Ltd.

1939. Stalin, J.V. *History of the Communist Party of the Soviet Union (Bolsheviks); Short Course.* Moscow, Foreign Languages Publishing House.

1942. Engels, Friedrich. *Herr Eugen Dühring's Revolution in Science (Anti-Dühring).* London, Lawrence & Wishart Ltd.

1942. Stalin, J.V. *Marxism and the National and Colonial Question.* London, Lawrence & Wishart Ltd.

1947. *Gazette of the Supreme Soviet.*

1947. Stalin, J.V. *Problems of Leninism.* Moscow, Foreign Language Publishing House.

1948. Vyshinsky, Andrei. *The Teachings of Lenin and Stalin on Proletarian Revolution and the State.* London, Soviet News.

1948. Vyshinksy, Andrei. *The Law of the Soviet State.* New York, The Macmillan Company.

1950. Stalin, J.V. *On the Draft Constitution of the USSR.* Moscow, Foreign Languages Publishing House.

1951. Marx, Karl and Engels, Friedrich. *Selected Works,* vol.i and ii. London, Lawrence & Wishart Ltd.

1953. Stalin, J.V. *Works,* vol.i. *Anarchism or Socialism?* London, Lawrence & Wishart Ltd.

1954. Stalin, J.V. *Works,* vol.ix. London, Lawrence & Wishart Ltd.

1954 Stalin, J.V. *Works,* vol.x. London, Lawrence & Wishart Ltd.

1955 Stalin, J.V. *Works,* vol.xiii. London, Lawrence & Wishart Ltd.

1955. Steinberg, Isaac. *In the Workshop of the Revolution.* London, Victor Gollancz Ltd.

1968. Engels, Friedrich, *The Role of Force in History*. London, Lawrence & Wishart Ltd.

1968. Ginzburg, Eugenia. *Into the Whirlwind*. London, Penguin.

1971. Mandelstam, Nadezhda. *Hope Against Hope: A Memoir*. London, Collins & Harvill Press.

1971, 1974. Krushchev, N. *Khrushchev Remembers* (2 vols.). London, Andre Deutsch.

1972. Stalin, J.V. *Economic Problems of Socialism in the USSR*. Moscow, Foreign Languages Publishing House.

1973. Stalin, J.V. *Concerning Marxism in Linguistics*. In Bruce Franklin. *The Essential Stalin. Major Theoretical Writings 1905-52*. London, Croom Helm.

1973/4. Solzhenitsyn, A. *The Gulag Archipelago 1918-1956*. London, Collins & Harvill Press.

1976. Marx, Karl and Engels, Friedrich. *Collected Works,* vol.iv. London, Lawrence & Wishart Ltd.

1978. *Constitution (Fundamental Law) of the Union of Soviet Socialist Republics*. Moscow, Novosti Press Agency Publishing House.

1979. Bukharin, Nikolai. *The Politics and Economics of the Transition Period*. London, Routledge & Kegan Paul.

1980. Pashukanis, Evgeny. *Selected Writings on Marxism and Law*. London, eds. Piers Beirne and Robert Sharlet. London, Academic Press.

1988. Stuchka, Pavel. *Selected Writings on Soviet Law and Marxism*. Eds. Robert Sharlet, Peter B. Maggs and Piers Beirne. London, M.E. Sharpe Publishers.

1993. Bukharin, Anna Larina. *This I Cannot Forget. The Memoirs of Bukharin's Widow*. London, Hutchinson.

1995. Stalin, J.V. *Letters to Molotov: 1925-36*. New Haven. Yale University Press.

2. Newspapers Journals and Reports

Hansard
Izvestia
Literary Russia
Pravda
Slavic Review
Thames TV
The London Times
The Russian Review
Trud (The Soviet trade union newspaper)

3. Secondary Sources

Anon. 1938. *The Letter of an Old Bolshevik: A Key to the Moscow Trials*. London, George Allen & Unwin Ltd.
Armstrong, John A. 1978. *Ideology, Politics, and Government in the Soviet Union*. New York, Praeger Publishers.

Babb, Hugh W. 1951. *Soviet Legal Philosophy*. Cambridge, Mass. Harvard University Press.

Beirne, P. and Quinney, R. 1982. *Marxism and Law.* New York, John Wiley & Sons.

Beirne, P. and Sharlet, R. 1968. Intro. in R. Conquest. 1968. *Justice and the Legal System in the USSR.* London, The Bodley Head.

Berdyaev, Nicolas. 1937. *The Origin of Russian Communism.* London, Geoffrey Bles: The Centenary Press.

Berg, Ger P. Van Den. 1985. *The Soviet System of Justice: Figures and Policy.* Dordrecht, Martinus Nijhoff Publishers.

Berman, Harold J. 1963. *Justice in the USSR. An Interpretation of Soviet Law.* Cambridge, Mass. Harvard University Press. 1966. *Soviet Criminal Law and Procedure: The RSFSR Codes.* Cambridge, Mass. Harvard University Press.

Boim, Leon and others. 1966. *Legal Controls in the Soviet Union.* Leyden, A.W. Sijthoff.

Bullock, Alan. 1991. *Hitler and Stalin: Parallel Lives.* London, Harper Collins.

Burbank, Jane. 1995. *Lenin and the Law in Revolutionary Russia. Slavic Review.* Cambridge, Mass. American Association for the Advancement of Slavic Studies, Inc.

Carr, E.H. 1964. *A History of Soviet Russia: The Bolshevik Revolution 1917-1923,* vol.1. London, Macmillan & Co. Ltd. *Socialism in One Country 1924-26.* London, Macmillan & Co. Ltd.

Channon, John. (ed.) 1998. *Politics, Society and Stalinism in the USSR.* London, Macmillan Press Ltd.

Coates, W.P. 1933. *The Moscow Trial (April, 1933).* London, The Anglo-Russian Parliamentary Committee.

Cohen, Stephen F. *Bukharin and the Bolshevik Revolution: A Political Biography 1888-1938.* Oxford, Oxford University Press.

Collins, Hugh. 1982. *Marxism and Law.* Oxford, Clarendon Press.

Conquest, Robert. (ed.) 1968. *Justice and the Legal System in the USSR*. London, The Bodley Head.

1970. *The Nation Killers: The Soviet Deportation of Nationalities*. London, Macmillan.

1971. *The Great Terror: Stalin's Purge of the Thirties*. London, Penguin Books.

1973. *The Great Terror: Revised edition*. London, Macmillan.

1986. *The Harvest of Sorrow*. London, Arrow Books.

1989. *Stalin and the Kirov Murder*. London, Hutchinson.

1990. *The Great Terror. A Reassessment*. London, Hutchinson.

D'Encausse, Hélène Carrère. 1981. *Stalin: Order through Terror*. London, Longmans.

Denisov, A. and Kirichenko, M. 1960. *Soviet State Law*. Moscow, Foreign Languages Publishing House.

Deutscher, Isaac. 1959. *The Prophet Unarmed: Trotsky 1921-1929*. London, Oxford University Press.

1966. *Stalin: A Political Biography*. London, Penguin Books.

Djilas, Milovan. 1969. *Conversations with Stalin*. Harmondsworth, Pelican Books.

Duranty, Walter. 1942. *The Kremlin and the People*. London, Hamish Hamilton.

Dziak, John. 1988. *Chekisty: A History of the KGB*. Lexington, Mass. Lexington Books.

Ellenstein, Jean. 1976. *The Stalin Phenomenon*. London, Lawrence & Wishart Ltd.

Fainsod, Merle. 1958. *Smolensk under Soviet Rule*. London, Macmillan.

1963. *How Russia is Ruled*. Cambridge Mass. Harvard University Press.

Figes, Orlando. 1996. *A People's Tragedy: The Russian Revolution 1891-1924*. London, Jonathan Cape.

Fischer, Louis. 1965. *The Life of Lenin*. London, Weidenfeld & Nicolson.

Fitzpatrick, Sheila. 1994. *Stalin's Peasants: Resistance and Survival in the Russian Village after Collectivization*. New York, Oxford University Press.

(ed.) 2000. *Stalinism: New directions*. London, Routledge.

Garros, Veronique (and others). 1995. *Intimacy and Terror: Soviet Diaries of the 1930s*. New York, The New Press.

Getty, J. Arch and Roberta T. Manning. (eds.) 1993. *Stalinist Terror: New Perspectives*. Cambridge, Cambridge University Press.

Getty, J. Arch and Oleg V. Naumov. 1999. *The Road to Terror: Stalin and the Self-Destruction of the Bolsheviks, 1932-1939*. New Haven, Yale University Press.

Hahn, Werner G. 1982. *Postwar Soviet Politics: The Fall of Zhdanov and the Defeat of Moderation, 1946-53*. London, Cornell University Press Ltd.

Hazard, John N. 1953. *Law and Social Change in the USSR*. London, Stevens & Sons Limited.

Hosking, Geoffrey. 1992. *A History of the Soviet Union 1917-1991*. London, Fontana.

Huskey, Eugene. 1987. *Vyshinsky, Krylenko, and the Shaping of the Soviet Legal Order*. Slavic Review. Cambridge, Mass. American Association for the Advancement of Slavic Studies, Inc.

Johnson, E.L. 1972. *An Introduction to the Soviet Legal System*. London, Methuen & Co. Ltd.

Katkov, George. 1969. *The Trial of Bukharin*. London, B.T. Batsford Ltd.

Kelsen, Hans. 1955. *The Communist Theory of Law.* London, Stevens & Sons Limited.

Kemp-Welch, A. (ed.) 1992. *The Ideas of Nicolai Bukharin.* Oxford, Clarendon Press.

Kolakowski, Leszek. 1978. *Main Currents of Marxism: Its Rise, Growth and Dissolution,* vol.ii, *The Golden Age* and vol.iii. *The Breakdown.* Oxford, Clarendon Press.

Konstantinovsky, Boris. 1953. *Soviet Law in Action. The Recollected Cases of a Soviet Lawyer.* Cambridge, Mass. Harvard University Press.

Kravchenko, Victor. 1947. *I Chose Freedom: The Personal and Political Life of a Soviet Official.* London, Robert Hale Ltd.

Kucherov, Samuel. 1970. *The Organs of Soviet Administration of Justice: Their History and Operation.* Leiden, E.J. Brill.

Leggett, George. 1981. *The Cheka: Lenin's Political Police.* Oxford, Clarendon Press.

Lewin, M. *Russian Peasants and Soviet Power.* 1968. London, George Allen & Unwin.

Makepeace, R.W. *Marxist Ideology and Soviet Criminal Law.* 1980. London. Croom Helm.

Mawdsley, Evan. 1998. *The Stalin Years: The Soviet Union 1929-1953.* Manchester, Manchester University Press.

McNeal, Robert H. 1988. *Stalin: Man and Ruler.* London, Macmillan Press.

Medvedev, Roy. 1979. *On Stalin and Stalinism.* Oxford, Oxford University Press.

1989. *Let History Judge: The Origins and Consequences of Stalinism.* New York, Columbia University Press.

Muggeridge, Malcolm. 1975. *Chronicle of Wasted Time.* Glasgow, Fontana/Collins.

Nove, Alec. 1964. *Was Stalin Really Necessary? Some Problems of Soviet Political Economy.* London, George Allen & Unwin.
1980. *An Economic History of the USSR.* London, Penguin.
1981. *Stalinism and After.* London, George Allen & Unwin.
Nove, Alec. (ed.) 1993. *The Stalin Phenomenon.* London, Weidenfield & Nicholson.

Orlov, Alexander. 1953. *The Secret History of Stalin's Crimes.* New York, Random House.

Phillips, Paul. 1980. *Marx and Engels on Law and Laws.* Oxford, Martin Robertson.
Pipes, Richard. 1986. *Legalized Lawlessness: Soviet Revolutionary Justice.* Institute for European Defence & Strategic Studies. London, Alliance Publishers Ltd.
1990. *The Russian Revolution, 1899-1919.* London, Harvill/ Harper Collins.
1994. *Russia Under the Bolshevik Regime: 1914-1924.* London, Harvill.
1996. *The Unknown Lenin from the Secret Archive.* New Haven, Yale University Press.
Polan, A.J. 1984. *Lenin and the End of Politics.* London, Methuen.
Pritt, D.N. 1933. *The Russian Legal System.* In Margaret I. Cole, *Twelve Studies in Soviet Russia.* London, Victor Gollancz Ltd.
1965. *Autobiography: From Right to Left.* (Part One). London, Lawrence & Wishart, Ltd.

Rigby, T.H. & Others (eds.) 1980. *Authority, Power and Policy in the USSR.* London, The Macmillan Press Ltd.

Schlesinger, Rudolph. 1945. *Soviet Legal Theory: Its Social Background and Development.* London, Kegan Paul, Trench, Trubner & Co. Ltd.

Service, Robert. 2000. *Lenin: A Biography*. London, Macmillan Publishers Limited.

Shachtman, Max. 1936. *Behind the Moscow Trial*. New York, Pioneer Publishers.

Shapiro, Leonard and Reddaway, Peter. (eds.) 1967. *Lenin, the Man, the Theorist, the Leader: A Reappraisal*. London, Pall Mall Press.

Solomon, Peter, Jr. 1978. *Soviet Criminologists and Criminal Policy: Specialists in Policy-Making*. London, The Macmillan Press Ltd.

1987. *Soviet Criminal Justice and the Great Terror*. Slavic Review. Cambridge, Mass. American Association for the Advancement of Slavic Studies, Inc.

1997. *Reforming Justice in Russia, 1864-1996: Power, Culture, and the Limits of Legal Order*. New York, M.E. Sharpe.

Solzhenitsyn, A. 1970. *One Day in the Life of Ivan Denisovich*. London, Gollancz.

1970. *The First Circle*. London, Fontana Press.

Swianiewicz, S. 1965. *Forced Labour and Economic Development: An Inquiry into the Experience of Soviet Industrialization*. London, Oxford University Press.

Sypnowich, Christine. 1990. *The Concept of Socialist Law*. Oxford, Clarendon Press.

Thurston, Robert W. 1996. *Life and Terror in Stalin's Russia: 1934-1941*. New Haven. Yale University Press.

Trotsky, Leon.1933. *The History of the Russian Revolution*, 3 vols. London, Victor Gollancz Ltd.

1946. *Stalin: An Appraisal of the Man and his Influence*. New York, Harper & Brothers.

1965. *The Revolution Betrayed: What is the Soviet Union and Where is it Going?* New York, Merit Publishers.

Tucker, Robert C. (ed.). 1965. *The Great Purge Trial*. New York. Grosset & Dunlap.
1973. *Stalin as Revolutionary 1879-1929*. A Study in History and Personality. New York, W.W. Norton & Company.
1977. (ed). *Stalinism: Essays in Historical Interpretation*. New York, W.W. Norton & Co.
1990. *Stalin in Power. The Revolution from Above. 1928-1941*. New York, W.W. Norton & Co.

Ulam, Adam B. 1974. *Stalin: The Man and his Era*. London, Allen Lane.

Ward, Chris. 1998. *The Stalinist Dictatorship*. London, Arnold.
1999. *Stalin's Russia*. London, Arnold.
Webb, Sidney and Beatrice. 1936. *Soviet Communism: A New Civilization?* London, Longmans.
Williams, Beryl. 1998. *Soviet historians and the rediscovery of the Soviet past*. In W. Lamont *Historical Controversies and Historians*. London, UCL Press.
2000. *Lenin*. Harlow, England, Longman.

Index